WRITING UP QUALITATIVE RESEARCH

HARRY F. WOLCOTT
University of Oregon

Qualitative Research Methods
Volume 20

SAGE PUBLICATION.
The International Professional Publishers
Newbury Park London New Delhi

For information address:

SAGE Publications, Inc.
2455 Teller Road
Newbury Park, California 91320

SAGE Publications Ltd.
6 Bonhill Street
London EC2A 4PU
United Kingdom

SAGE Publications India Pvt. Ltd.
M-32 Market
Greater Kailash I
New Delhi 110 048 India

Printed in the United States of America

Library of Congress Cataloging-in-Publication Data

Wolcott, Harry F., 1929-
Writing up qualitative research / Harry F. Wolcott.
p. cm. — (Qualitative research methods : v. 20)
Includes bibliographical references.
ISBN 0-8039-3792-X. — ISBN 0-8039-3793-8 (pbk.)
1. Technical writing. 2. Research—Authorship. I. Title.
II. Series.
T11.W65 1990
808'.0666—dc20 90-8272
CIP

95 96 97 98 99 10 9

Sage Production Editor: Susan McElroy

CONTENTS

If I lived twenty more years and was able to work, how I should have to modify the *Origin*, and how much the views on all points will have to be modified! Well it is a beginning, and that is something. . . .

Charles Darwin to J. D. Hooker, 1869

EDITORS' INTRODUCTION

Social research is both a process and a product. Presumably, one informs the other. Of the two, the process of research has received by far the most attention from practitioners and critics alike. Recently, however, the product of research — the written account — has emerged as a topic in its own right and, as investigators of the text point out, the relationship between words and worlds is anything but easy or transparent. Moreover, convincing accounts turn in part on the respect an author shows for certain narrative or genre conventions that in given periods and given fields define the "proper" reporting style for a particular form of research. Yet, despite the confidence of some readers who apparently are able to recognize the good from the bad account (at 50 paces), the narrative conventions respected and/or bent by social researchers remain largely implicit and undercoded in the method literature.

Harry F. Wolcott takes up these textual matters in the 20th Volume of the Sage Series on Qualitative Research Methods. Drawing on his own authorial experience, he begins his exploration of the qualitative research process at the point where most method texts leave off — with the writing process itself. Central to his approach is a commitment to remain in touch with materials gathered in the field such that textual claims and interpretive perspectives can be illustrated well by data collected for just these purposes. One cannot create an ethnography, for example, unless one has done intensive fieldwork. The tricks of the writing trade are, in Harry Wolcott's view, very much dependent on the nature of the research experience itself.

The importance of *Writing Up Qualitative Research* lies in the author's direct and candid treatment of the writing problems faced by social researchers, novice and veteran. Some of these problems are conceptual and deal with the nature of social understanding. Some are practical and deal with reporting formats, authorial voice, use of language, and presentational devices. All of these problems involve choice, however, and helping authors make good choices is what this text is all about. There is much to learn here as Harry Wolcott takes us from the hurly-burly of the field to the quiet workroom where a researcher's quest necessarily must draw to a close—if only temporarily—with the steady inscription of words onto the page.

—John Van Maanen
Peter K. Manning
Marc L. Miller

WRITING UP QUALITATIVE RESEARCH

HARRY F. WOLCOTT
University of Oregon

1. READING ABOUT WRITING

I hope this idea works: me writing about writing instead of getting on with my own; you reading what someone else has to say about writing instead of getting on with yours. Most of what I have learned about writing up qualitative research is the result of doing it, along with some careful—and carefully meted out—suggestions from helpful critic-readers along the way. I appreciate being told that I am a good writer (by academic standards, not literary ones, of course) but the cold, hard fact is that I am not. A claim I can make is that I care about my writing; I work diligently at it. What others read are final drafts, not first ones. Pride and perseverance must substitute for talent.

How about my title for this little monograph? Did it reach out and grab you? If you never gave it a thought, maybe this is the book for you. If the title immediately set you to wondering whether anything helpful can be learned from someone who writes "up" (don't most people write "down"?), or uses a four-word title when three might have sufficed, then you already may be sufficiently word- and style-conscious about many of the things I have to say.

This is not a manual on style, however. Style is part of the writing process; I will add what I can or, more often, reiterate advice that seasoned authors have offered for years. My purpose is to help with the critical task of ensuring that whatever you have written down in the way of field notes from observations, interviews, or archival research gets written up into a final account, and written so well that your qualitative study is also a quality one. I have written not for professional writers but for professionals who must write—not those of you who delight in the art of personal expression, but those of you who write because others expect you to contribute to the literature in your field.

You may find my style casual, perhaps disconcerting at times. I try to write in a straightforward and unpretentious manner and, in presuming to write about writing, I may have gone overboard in my effort to be informal rather than didactic. What I have done in my attempt to help you organize and write up your accounts is to tell you how I go about organizing and writing up mine, and to share ideas gleaned from others. Straight talk, writer to writer.

So much for "writing up." From my title you know that the focus is on writing up *research.* As authors are advised to do, I have written with a particular audience in mind: people who engage in what has come to be known as qualitative or descriptive or naturalistic research. This "naturalistic paradigm," as it has been called, is known by numerous other labels as well. Researchers Yvonna Lincoln and Egon Guba (1985, p. 7) have identified several prominent aliases for the term *naturalistic:* postpositivistic, ethnographic, phenomenological, subjective, case study, qualitative, hermeneutic, humanistic. Those of you who pursue these or closely related approaches are my audience. You constitute a special subset of field-oriented researchers who not only work in a broad qualitative vein (along with biographers, historians, and philosophers) but often apply the very label *qualitative* or *qualitative/descriptive* to your research, in contrast to those who specify that they are doing biography, history, or philosophy.

Dear reader (as chapters written in my grandmother's generation sometimes began), I realize that you have no opportunity to tell me why you chose this book, what kind of information would be most helpful to you, or where you would like me to begin. I must more or less make you up as I go along, trying to anticipate what brings you to this reading and to address those concerns. More important, just as in lecturing, I must also try to convince you that I know what I'm talking about, so that you will attend to a discussion of my problems and solutions and not remain too preoccupied with your own. I must engage you through a monologue in which I do the talking. No wonder ethnographer Richard Warren once described writing as "an act of arrogance" (I wonder what he thinks about colleagues who presume to tell others how to go about it?). Yet for both your sake and mine, I prefer writing to lecturing. Here you can put me down without letting me down; if you fall asleep, I need never know.

You do think of yourself as a writer, don't you? Or are you an ought-to-be-writing writer, or worse, an ought-to-be-researching researcher who simply can't get started? You are among the latter if you realize that you need to publish but find yourself at a loss even for a research topic. This is frequently a problem for recent Ph.D.s who accept university "teaching" assignments in professional schools and applied fields only to find—as they suspected all along—that advancement depends on "scholarly production" instead. That means writing!

The reason behind my hunch that some ought-to-be-writing types are lurking out there is that with the growing acceptance of qualitative approaches to research in recent years—in such diverse fields as business, economic development, education, international aid, leisure studies, nursing, physical education, public health, and social psychology—academics have been turning to qualitative research out of desperation as well as inspiration. Having reached a stage in their careers when they are expected to publish, these professionals suddenly find themselves inadequately prepared to conduct research. They look for ways to become what they believe they must become: instant researchers. Qualitative approaches beckon because they appear easy or natural. And were it not for the complexity of conceptualizing qualitative studies, conducting the research, analyzing it, and writing it up, perhaps they would be.

Although this monograph is directed to a particular subset of researchers, I trust that there are helpful suggestions here for all inquiry-oriented writing. Keep in mind, however, that my focus is on qualitative/descriptive research and on processes related to getting it written up, rather than on related facets—for example, conceptualizing, conducting the fieldwork, and analyzing—despite the fact that these processes are virtually inseparable. Further, and perhaps disappointing to some readers, you will find a mechanical cast to much of the advice I offer. Instead of wheedling you to attempt great leaps of intuitive insight, you are more likely to find me arguing in favor of pedestrian coding and sorting to construct a solid study one brick at a time.

My assumption is that anyone who can see a way to proceed from the "top down," introducing an overarching concept, unifying theme, or persistent paradox, will do just that. If you know what you're about, get on with it! If you do not know what you're about, you may need to proceed with considerably less flair (and risk) and to work from the "bottom up." The suggestions I propose—ranging from when and where to begin (in Chapter 2) to what to include in an appendix (in

Chapter 5), can be regarded not so much as the best way to do things as ways to get around thinking that you can't. I don't follow all these suggestions myself. Some I have tried but no longer use, a few seem like good ideas to pass along although I have never tried them, and some points are raised merely to review the range of opinion or practice extant. I have included an immodest number of references to my own writing, in some instances to avoid repeating myself but more often because they are the studies I know best. I wrote them to be read, and I take every opportunity to call attention to them.

I also trust you realize that a brief monograph like this does not presume to be the *Compleat Guide to Writing Up Qualitative Research.* For example, a vigorous dialogue has begun about descriptive research as text and the role of critical analysis in the social sciences, but these issues are not addressed here. Neither do I discuss underlying issues of theory in my effort to stay with the immediate task of helping you to get your thoughts and observations into presentable written form. Pretty basic stuff, all rather obvious to anyone who has completed the write-up of a study, found a way to get the results published, and suffered no ill aftereffects (e.g., a satisfactory dissertation but an unsatisfactory experience writing it, or a devastating review too early in one's career). At the same time, none of this is obvious at all to anyone who has faltered along the way; become bogged down by words, data, or theory; or who feels both underprepared and overwhelmed at the prospect of ever starting.

Nor is this going to be *Writing Made Fun.* Writing is always challenging and sometimes satisfying, but that is about as far as I can go in singing its praises. I confess to having become hooked: writing is the most satisfying scholarly activity in which I engage, and the most visibly lasting. Nevertheless, a few rare moments of ecstasy over something well written or favorably reviewed are meager compensation for all the agony endured to achieve it. The important thing for each of us is that when we have something to write about, the writing gets done.

This monograph serves as a case in point. I accepted the invitation to prepare it because I felt I might help struggling researcher-writers get on with their writing by describing some tactics that have worked for me. I began thinking about the project and jotting notes literally from the moment the idea was first proposed. I soon found time to begin organizing and writing a first draft. More than 15 months later, I submitted what proved to be the first of several "final" versions. Clearly one is at an advantage when invited to prepare a manuscript on an appropriate topic, and I am at a stage in my career when I can write what I choose. But no one could tell me exactly what story to tell or how to proceed. Those are the responsibilities of an author. I was promised only an interested editorial eye; there are no huge advances or guaranteed contracts for academic publishing of such modest scope.

I hope you share my belief that writing well is neither a luxury nor an option in reporting qualitative research; it is absolutely essential. Throughout the text, I stress the importance of revising and editing, something all aspiring authors can do (and ought to do more). Careful editing is the antidote for the lack of giftedness among the huge corpus of us who recognize that we had better write but are not among the better writers. There is little point to our efforts if we cannot get anyone to read what we have to report.

A writing tip borrowed from Lewis Carroll's *Alice's Adventures in Wonderland:* When you come to the end, stop. I have said enough by way of introduction. Nobody minds short chapters, especially when there are longer ones ahead.

2. GETTING GOING

This chapter presumes to help you get started with writing. "Getting Going," by the way, is a terrible title that offends my ear and, I hope, offends yours as well. If it does, there's hope for you as an editor of your own material, catching phrases during the rewriting process that somehow slip by the first or second time.

Some questions that come to mind for organizing this chapter relate to sorting and organizing data; focusing; and deciding where, when, and how to begin. I will touch upon each of these facets. Let me begin with some practical considerations for getting you started.

How To Begin

At the moment you generate sentences that could conceivably appear in your completed account, you have begun your writing. Whether your earliest efforts survive your subsequent pruning and editing is quite another matter and not of major consequence; you can look anyone in the eye and state that your writing is actually under way. There are all kinds of fancy words you can use to describe what you are doing prior to writing—organizing, conceptualizing, outlining, mulling, or "cranking-up," as Peter Woods (1985, pp. 92-97) describes it—but until your pencil forms sentences on paper or you achieve the equivalent effect through some miracle of modern technology you have no basis for claiming either the sympathy or admiration of your family, friends, or colleagues that you are *really* writing.

In addition to having something of consequence to write about, the basic requirements for getting at the task are a time and place and, depending on your personal style and the well-formedness of your thoughts, either an idea (to develop for yourself) or a plan (in which case you can start writing for your intended audience). Be discerning about the minimum conditions you require to sustain your writing. For example, although I *prefer* to have an adequate supply of Triscuits and cheese on hand while writing, they are not absolute necessities. On the other hand, I cannot write with real—or even threatened—distraction; uninterrupted quiet is essential.

For productive scholarship, I find working at home far more satisfactory than trying to accomplish anything at my university office, a place of incessant interruption. For some colleagues, home does not provide sanctuary; instead, they learn to use their offices productively by carefully protecting or scheduling their writing time. Students who must do their writing apart from either home or office seem to survive, so a practical bit of advice is that if you don't have a natural workplace for writing, then create or commandeer one. When I must work on campus without interruption, I gather up my materials and head for the library, but I choose a spot in the library—or even a different library (the law library, the science library)—where neither the books nor their readers offer much distraction.

I enjoy showing houseguests my wonderful new study—a large, attractive room with a high countertop and drafting stool (I like to be "up" and sometimes stand rather than sit as I work), a lovely vista of trees and hills through the constant light of north-facing windows, my professional library just steps away. But these are accoutrements of age and status, not prerequisites. Much of my writing has been done with Bic pens on lined yellow pads and at a cleared kitchen counter or table, especially during periods of field research conducted far from my accustomed work station.

Given a choice, I prefer to write where I can spread before me (and leave undisturbed) the materials I want immediately at hand, including a dictionary or two and an extra tablet for jotting down thoughts or working through a complex phrase or idea before committing it to the manuscript. In spite of the inconvenience of having to "clear your desk" each mealtime, even if you eat all your meals at home the kitchen table ought to be free for about 22 hours out of every 24, making it one possibility. Plus, the coffee pot—and Triscuits—are conveniently nearby. Some questions have been raised about whether caffeine is a stimulant to creative thinking, and perhaps you should restrict heavy coffee drinking to getting you through routine tasks such as retyping or keying handwritten sections into the computer. My point is not really about coffee and Triscuits, however. I'm suggesting that you inventory your writing-related idiosyncrasies and assess their importance to you. Pamper yourself. What does it take to get you to sit down to write; to keep you productively, even happily, engaged at it; and to ensure that you will return? Given realistic options, what is your best workable combination of time and place?

Set as much routine as possible to make the most of the precious time available for writing, for there will never be enough. Buffer against interruption. Make yourself sufficiently comfortable that you look forward to your writing time rather than dread the thought. I attend to chair and table heights, chair comfort, light, air circulation, and room temperature. I like adequate space for the ever-expanding body of materials I want close at hand. When I realized years ago that I tended to bring my work to the kitchen counter after breakfast rather than go to my study, and that it was the *height* of the counter and kitchen stools that I found so accommodating, at my first opportunity I designed a new study with a built-in countertop even a bit higher (39") than the customary kitchen counter.

I was amused to read in Howard Becker's neat little book *Writing for Social Scientists* (1986) that most of us perform some ritual either as a final act of avoidance or as a physical marker for getting started with the day's writing. Some of his students—and some of mine—reveal that they shower, sharpen pencils, or vacuum prior to writing and, as one student noted, "There's always the ironing." A new breed who appear able to sit in front of a monitor and go right to work are recognizing that the inherent playfulness of computers offers a whole new set of distractions ("computer fritters" as Jeffrey Nash, 1990, refers to them) that can divert the attention of author/researchers with consequences more devastating than the computer viruses that attack their programs. My own warming-up ritual is to clear my desk, a functional behavior if I literally push things aside in order to give full and immediate attention to writing, but an obvious diversion when attending to details encroaches on time supposedly reserved for writing.

I assess the true importance each of us gives to writing by the priority we assign it in terms of competing options and responsibilities. My optimum time is immediately after breakfast, with the promise of several uninterrupted hours. I regard myself as "really writing" when writing gets prime time and top priority. The important thing is not that writing must occur first, but that it receives first priority in the day's activities. A good test of commitment is whether you are able to ignore the telephone's ring or, if others will answer on your behalf, to have them explain that you are unavailable because you are writing. I assume that night writers make difficult choices when members of the household review the evening television fare, particularly the specials. Might you videotape them and reward yourself later?

In terms of organizing, I identify three key ingredients that collectively comprise what I will call The Plan. At least two aspects of The Plan need to be written out, not floating about in one's head. The first is a *statement of purpose.* You have your purpose well in mind when you can draft a critical, clear, and concise sentence that begins, "The purpose of this study (chapter, monograph, article) is . . ." Although structurally this is a most uninteresting beginning, I know of no better way to help academic writers find, declare, and maintain a focus than to have this sentence up front, not only in their minds but in their manuscripts. I am impressed by authors who are able to get the message across more creatively, but the creative rewriting can come later. In any writing over which I exert an influence (as dissertation director, journal editor, or colleague) I make a strong case not only for putting that flat-footed statement of purpose into the text but also for making it sentence number one of paragraph number one of chapter number one.

The second critical element of The Plan is a *detailed written outline or sequence.* Schooling ruined formal outlining for me, with all the misplaced attention to indenting, numbering, and rigid rules of unknown origin (e.g., you can't have just one item in a subset; there must be at least two). But the purposes accomplished by an outline are exactly what I need: an orderly progression, a clear identification of major points and subordinate ones, and an overview to allow me to assess whether the structure I have designed accommodates the data to be presented and provides an appropriate sequence for the presentation. The essential element here is the *sequence,* not the act of putting it on paper. I recognize that some seasoned fieldworkers insist that they carry their studies around in their heads, committing no prior outline to paper. After you are properly seasoned, you may want to try it. Not at first.

Developing an expanded table of contents accomplishes the same purpose as an outline. Preparing a table of contents also feels more like writing than outlining does, particularly for material requiring several major sections. Tables of contents also are free from the constraints of formal outlining. I am so convinced of their value as a way to organize any major writing project that I ask my doctoral students to include a tentative table of contents in their dissertation proposals. Proposals ordinarily are prepared before the research has begun, so the usual reaction is, "How can I possibly provide a table of contents when I haven't even started the research?" Unbowed, I also note that I'd like them to estimate the number of pages they plan to devote to each chapter.

The lesson is different from what students expect. Their first attempts often reveal more rigidity in their perception of the structure of a dissertation than actually exists. For example, although chapter two is a favorite spot for the traditional literature review, there is no ironclad rule—even in the otherwise totally inflexible graduate school at my university—that chapter two *must* be a literature review. Nor is there any rule insisting that one chapter be devoted to that topic at all. I expect my students to know the relevant literature, but I do not want them to lump (dump?) it all into a chapter that remains unconnected to the rest of the study. I want them to draw upon the literature selectively and appropriately as needed in the telling of their story. In our descriptive and analytic accounts, the most appropriate place for examining the literature seems to me to be in consort with the analysis of new data. Ordinarily this calls for introducing related research toward the end of a study rather than at the beginning, except for the necessary "nesting" of the problem in the introduction.

Another benefit of assigning a seemingly arbitrary number of pages to a nonexistent chapter in a hypothetical table of contents is that students realize they *do* have a sense of the manuscript they expect to develop. Making an estimate proves not so absurd after all. Descriptive studies often exceed reasonable expectations for length. Anticipating and proportioning the account not only helps to give a sense of the piece as a whole but may prevent overwriting in introductory sections such as "Method" or "Significance of the Problem" that eventually must compete for space with the critical descriptive/analytical mass.

The expense of copying multiple drafts of a lengthy study gives real meaning to and incentive for an economy of words for students inclined toward lengthy dissertations. Little do they realize they are not likely ever again to be free to set their own limits. Journal editors specify maximum lengths and almost invariably return manuscripts with the comment, "Needs to be cut." Book review editors give their assignments in terms of maximum numbers of *words*. Publishers typically tell authors how long their books can be, although conventional wisdom suggests it should be the other way around. My instructions for preparing this monograph, *if* I wished to have it considered for the Qualitative Research Methods Series, were to observe "a strict limit of 100-120 double-spaced *manuscript* pages, which translates to 80-90 printed pages."

By the time one identifies as major and minor headings those matters that must be addressed (e.g., Introduction, Method, Description, Analysis, Summary and Implications), and assigns seemingly arbitrary numbers of pages to everything but the chapter(s)-of-unknown-length reserved for Description and Analysis, the message is clear and clearly different from what one might have expected: space is limited. Given the level of detail ordinarily found in qualitative studies, how can adequate descriptive material be included?

For qualitative studies based on observational or interview data, projecting a table of contents complete with estimated chapter lengths leads to one of the most important and paradoxical circumstances of our work: The major problem we face in qualitative inquiry is not to get data, but to get rid of it! With writing comes the always painful task (at least from the standpoint of the person who gathered it) of winnowing material to a manageable length, communicating only the essence rather than exhibiting the bulky catalogues that testify to one's painstaking thoroughness. The greater our commitment to letting informants provide their own interpretations of meanings and events—the *emic* emphasis, as it is known in anthropological circles—the greater the proclivity to provide lengthy accounts that can cost us the enthusiasm not only of readers but of potential publishers as well. The lengthier the study, the more costly to produce it and, correspondingly, the greater the risk that it will not attract a wide readership.

The third and final element of The Plan need not be written out but does need to be carefully thought out: *Determine the basic story you are going to tell, who is to do the telling, and what representational style you will follow for joining observer and observed.* (See the extended discussion of three narrative conventions for reporting qualitative studies—realist, confessional, and impressionist—in John Van Maanen's splendid monograph *Tales of the Field: On Writing Ethnography,* 1988.) This question of authorial voice can be critical in qualitative research. In approaches that focus on the life of one or a few individuals, the problem is compounded when informants are capable of telling their stories themselves, raising doubts about how or whether we should make our own presence known.

In quantitatively oriented approaches, and among the more self-consciously "scientific" qualitative types as well, researchers typically desert their subjects at the last minute, leaving folks and findings alike to fend for themselves, seemingly untainted by human hands and most certainly untouched by human hearts. One of the opportunities—and challenges—posed by qualitative approaches is to regard our fellow humans as people instead of subjects, and to regard ourselves as humans who conduct our research *among* rather than *on* them. Fieldworkers usually find it more efficient to assume the role of narrator than to present an entire account through informants' own words (notable exceptions include such classics as Leo Simmons's *Sun Chief,* 1942; or Oscar Lewis's *The Children of Sanchez,* 1961). There is a preference, however, for letting informants render the narrative part of the account in their own words, particularly in life histories (e.g., Crapanzano, 1980; Shostak, 1981; for an article-length example, see Wolcott, 1983a).

Because the researcher's role is ordinarily such an integral part of qualitative study, I write descriptive accounts in the first person, and I urge that others do (or, in some cases, be allowed to do) the same. I recognize that there are still academics and academic editors on the loose who insist that research be reported in the third person. I recently had a journal submission edited into impersonal third-person language without my permission and without the editor informing me. I think the practice reveals a belief that impersonal language presupposes objective truth. Science may be better served by substituting *participants* for *we,* or *the observer* for *I,* but I have yet to be convinced that our highest calling is to serve science (see Wolcott, 1990b). Perhaps a more compelling case can be made on behalf of matching the formality of the writing with the formality of the approach. The more critical the observer's role and subjective assessment, the more important to have that role and presence acknowledged in the reporting.

When To Begin

Hear this: *You cannot begin writing early enough.* And yes, I really mean it. Would that mean you might write a first draft before ever venturing into the field to begin observations or interviews? Correct. Read on.

I have come to the (admittedly oversimplified) belief that people whose lives are involved closely with the printed page can be sorted into two major categories: those who read and those who write. Obviously many literate folk do neither, and a few do both. In the main, however, my impression is that people whose occupations require continual engagement with written words gravitate toward the extremes. They become preoccupied either with consuming words or producing them. How about you: essentially a reader, or essentially a writer?

I confess that my dichotomy may be little more than rationalization, for I do not consider myself a reader. I do not mean that I do not read; rather, in a world of readers (teachers, researchers, and students), and relatively speaking, I am neither a voracious reader nor am I particularly well-read. I must, and do, read thousands and thousands of pages a year: student papers; dissertations; reports; manuscripts and proposals sent by publishers, colleagues, funding agencies, and tenure review committees; professional journals and texts (thank goodness for book reviews); and the newspapers, magazines, and books one reads in the effort—or pretense—to keep up. Most of my reading is professional and most of my professional reading is tedious. I rarely read for pleasure, and never for "relaxation." I did not enroll in the classic literature courses as an undergraduate; I doubted that I would be able to read fast enough, or get what I was supposed to get out of such reading. Four decades later, my reading in the classics is still remedial. I remember a colleague who taught American literature describe how he broke into a cold sweat whenever he walked into any well-stocked university bookstore (in the old days, when they stocked books where the T-shirts, greeting cards, and computers are now) to be reminded once more of reading yet to be done. I sometimes experience that same feeling at the arrival of publishers' announcements or another issue of one of the journals in which I try to remain current.

I read what I must; I write whenever I can. That probably explains why I find field research so appealing: I can be engaged actively in the research process, seeing and hearing and pondering it all for myself rather than getting it secondhand. I do not envy colleagues whose research forays take them only to the library. Not surprisingly, I regard my most effective reading as reading done in tandem with writing—that is, purposeful reading (and casual reading as well) done while I am engaged in fieldwork and/or preparing a manuscript. Writing gives purpose and focus to searching for new sources and reviewing old ones, another instance in which the real trick is not to get, but to get rid of, extraneous material so that what remains is manageable.

The conventional wisdom is that writing reflects thinking. I am drawn to a different position: Writing *is* thinking—or, stated more cautiously, writing is a form of thinking (see Becker, 1986, p. ix, who in turn cites Flower, 1979; Flower and Hayes, 1981). Writers who indulge themselves by waiting until their thoughts are "clear" run the risk of never starting at all. And that, as Becker explains, is why it is "so important to write a draft rather than to keep on preparing and thinking about what you will write when you start" (Becker, 1986, p. 56). Writing is a great way to discover what we are thinking, as well as to discover gaps in our thinking. Unfortunately, that means we must be prepared to catch ourselves red-handed when we seem not to be thinking at all. The fact should not escape us that when the writing is not going well, we probably have nothing (yet) to say; most certainly we are not yet able to say it.

This is the point at which readers and writers part company. Readers compulsively want more; they cannot know enough. They have difficulty addressing the writing task until the "knowing" is complete, which it never is. Readers are intellectually honest. They deserve our respect, our understanding, perhaps even our sympathy. Their easily recognized counterparts among fieldworkers are those who falter as fieldwork deadlines draw near, insisting that they still don't have enough to begin the write-up. The familiar rationale has an admirable note of humility: "I'm not quite ready."

Recall Richard Warren's characterization of writing as an act of arrogance? Can you force yourself to enter into arrogance and begin to write in spite of the fact that you do not yet know as much as you feel you ought to know? Are the words of Clifford Geertz sufficiently encouraging, that it is "not necessary to know everything in order to understand something" (Geertz, 1973, p. 20)? If your answer is that you need to consult six more volumes in the library—or spend six more months in the field—before you will be ready, you may possess an enviable capacity for thoroughness, but I have doubts about you as a writer. Can you sit down immediately (why not today?) and turn your hand to writing? No need even to finish reading this monograph just now. (If you're browsing in the bookstore, however, you may want to purchase it to read later. Otherwise, won't you always wonder how it ends?)

A suggestion I now make to anyone contemplating a qualitative/descriptive study, and especially to anyone who expresses concern about writing before the research itself has begun, is this: *Write a preliminary draft of the study. Then begin the research.*

I did not say to show the draft to anyone, but I earnestly believe you cannot begin writing too early. Virtually everyone who writes about writing offers the same advice. Hear Milton Lomask's counsel to would-be biographers: "Irrespective of where your research stands, start the writing the minute some of the material begins coming together in your mind. . . . Get the words down. You can always change them" (1987, pp. 26-27).

Writing a draft before beginning fieldwork has some great advantages. First, like the proposed-table-of-contents exercise described earlier, it is a good reminder about format, sequence, space limitations, and focus. Second, it forces you to establish a baseline for your work, just as you will eventually reveal to others your end point for it. You will have documented what you believe to be the case, making a matter of record certain biases and assumptions that otherwise might prove conveniently flexible and accommodating had they remained as abstractions. Finally, you will begin a systematic inventory of what you already know, what you need to know, and what you are looking for.

We all know (or believe) far more than we realize about virtually any topic of professional interest. Writing is a way to gain access to that personal fund of information. Conversing with colleagues is another. It is flattering on occasion to have someone say, "I'd like to try out an idea on you." But those of us in the word business are pretty slick; we can talk ourselves out of a non sequitur almost as smoothly as we can trap ourselves in one. Writing offers a private way to capture and give concrete form to sometimes too-elusive ideas.

Do I follow this practice myself? Yes, in somewhat modified fashion. Except for my initiation into long-term fieldwork—my dissertation study of a Kwakiutl Indian village and school, from which I returned without the least idea of how to proceed with the writing—I have always turned to writing early. Writing offers a way of tracking what I have understood and discerning what I need to find out next. Early writing also presupposes a willingness to let go of words as easily as you generate them, however, and that I find hard to do. Therefore, my advice for anyone hesitant about writing is to begin immediately, but my own practice is to delay as long as possible the moment when I begin drafting sentences. I focus my effort on an immediately prior stage that I call "tight outlining": getting sources, concepts, examples, sequence, and everything else lined up and ready to go. I don't worry whether I can get something on paper; I know I can. If you do not share that same sense of confidence, start earlier.

With obvious gradations between them, there are two different approaches to "getting going" with writing. The recommended strategy for anyone whose style has not yet evolved is simply to let the words flow—to the extreme of making no corrections, checking no spelling or references, not even rereading once you find yourself on a roll (see Becker, 1986, chapter 3; for elaboration on a technique known as *freewriting*—forcing yourself to "write without stopping for ten minutes"—see Elbow, 1981, pp. 13ff.). With the miracle of word processing so easily at hand and so forgiving about mistakes and changes (with easy deletions, screen preview, and cut-and-paste features), freewriting becomes feasible for everyone. Whether you prefer to "talk" (or freewrite) only to yourself, systematically to save all your bits and pieces for later review, or compulsively to pursue every idea to final prose form, your computer awaits your command.

A drawback of the amazing new word processing programs, however, has become evident in my reading of student papers (and, occasionally, colleagues' papers as well). The ease of production often results in faster rather than better writing. Capabilities for easy revision often are ignored. Hastily written and hastily proofed first drafts are tendered as final copy; printout is equated with "in print," the sketch proffered in lieu of the careful rendering.

Student writing is probably the worst preparation for learning to write well, and writing a dissertation usually snuffs out any remaining spark of creativity. Student writing most often is done on a hurried, one-shot basis, with neither time nor motivation for the reflection and revisions that lead to better writing. The entire process of drafting and revising is short-circuited in the tasks and timelines confronting students. We want them to become accomplished writers, but do not provide opportunities for them to practice what we have discovered necessary to accomplish it. (As a remedy, I have begun offering an "early bird" option in some classes. Students who can meet an advanced deadline may submit a working draft of their term papers for critical review two weeks before the assignment is due.)

An opposite approach from those who begin by freewriting is followed by writers sometimes known as "bleeders." I do not know the origin of the term, although it brings to mind an observation attributed to sports journalist Red Smith: "There's nothing to writing. All you do is sit down at a typewriter and open a vein." Bleeders are methodical. Their approach reflects a combination of confidence and command about the writing process, along with some personal qualities (hang-ups?) about having everything just right. They worry over each line. They do not continue with the next sentence until the present one is perfected. Once correctly set, however, a sentence is viewed pretty much as a finished product. In the old days, bleeders usually wrote with pencil or pen to facilitate crossouts and interlining (squeezing corrections between existing lines).

Bleeders tend to be slow writers, but they get the job done. Often they set a number of words or pages as their daily objective, such as Peter Woods's "standard 'production rate' of five written pages, or a thousand words a day" (1985, p. 93). Most of us fare better by committing ourselves to blocks of time rather than to a fixed number of pages. In writing up qualitative research, page production can prove a deceptive goal; one might draft 10 pages of descriptive narrative one day and struggle with 10 sentences of interpretation on another. Nevertheless, if you recognize the bleeder in your own style, and you cannot imagine yourself romping through an early draft and subsequently discarding material with abandon, then perhaps a tightly detailed outline (or table of contents) is enough to get you started on the slow-but-steady production of a first draft.

Most likely you will shift back and forth between these two approaches. This may depend on mood and energy level, but is more likely to reflect the type of material you are writing and your previous experience. My writing sometimes flows easily, yet may suddenly slow to a snail's pace during efforts at making sense or proposing interpretation. The extremes are easy to recognize – when the words don't come easily, I leave the computer keyboard and retreat to my Bic pens and yellow pads to push words onto paper one at a time.

In *Writing for Social Scientists,* Howard Becker has a chapter seductively titled "One Right Way" (1986, chapter 3). His point, as any experienced writer will recognize immediately, is that there is no such thing. For his comparable chapter in *Writing With Power,* author Peter Elbow takes no risk that anyone might misunderstand; his title is "The Dangerous Method: Trying to Write It Right the First Time" (1981, chapter 6). Whatever combination of steps and strategies that works for you is "right" as long as ideas are put to paper so that subsequently they can be transformed into the coherent statement destined eventually to become a final draft.

Where To Begin

If you can sit down and write a first draft of a study before beginning systematic new research, then writing is already joined to your research and you are in the catbird seat. What we say should happen in qualitative studies really does happen when progressive problem setting and focus, fieldwork and analysis, move forward in complementary fashion and the writing proceeds as an integral part of the fully orchestrated research process. But don't expect the parts to come together that easily. If good results could be achieved effortlessly, there wouldn't be so many books and courses about writing or audiences anxious to have the secrets and recipes revealed.

Suppose you are a conservative type who takes seriously the opportunity inherent in qualitative research for exploration and discovery. You begin with a broadly defined purpose, acknowledging that you are not sure exactly what you are looking for. To convince yourself of your objectivity, you steadfastly refuse even to acknowledge your hunches, suspicions, or—to use Malinowski's (1922/1984, p. 9) well-known phrase—"foreshadowed problems." Only when the fieldwork seems virtually complete do you feel it appropriate to turn your attention to writing. (Too bad, really. Malinowski himself suggested [p. 13] that the writing should begin earlier, through a "constant interplay of constructive attempts and empirical checking.")

Where to begin the writing task? Returning to advice from *Alice's Adventures in Wonderland,* you might begin at the beginning, continue until you reach the end, and then stop. This may be good advice for how the completed work should read, but it is not necessarily good advice for writers preparing their first qualitative study. I can suggest two alternatives to beginning at the beginning. (There is yet another, which is to start with the conclusion. If you can start there, however, either you are an old hand at this or you have confused writing up qualitative research with finding support for a position paper. If your research seems to prove that you were right all along, you may be conducting social reform under the guise of social research!)

One way to begin is to write about method, situating your approach within an appropriate body of literature and then describing how you went about your study. Your discussion about method can be drafted early and separately. Later, it can be plugged into the final manuscript in one of several spots: as part of the introduction, as a separate chapter in a monograph or dissertation, or as an appendix.

But don't plan to devote a substantial portion of your account to discussing method; if you have that much to say, write it up separately. Give your attention to the substance of your research. In the last two decades, qualitative methods—which in many instances would be portrayed more accurately as qualitative techniques—have come to be widely known and accepted. There is no longer a call for each researcher to discover and defend them anew, nor a need to provide an exhaustive review of the literature about such standard procedures as participant observation or interviewing. Instead of having to describe and defend qualitative approaches, as we once felt obligated to do, it is often difficult to say anything new or startling about them. Neophyte researchers who only recently have experienced these approaches first-hand need to recognize that their audiences probably do not share a comparable sense of excitement about hearing them described once again.

In 1966, I began the fieldwork reported in *The Man in the Principal's Office: An Ethnography* (Wolcott, 1973/1984). A year later, while continuing with the fieldwork on a more limited basis, I began writing. Not only did I begin by writing the method chapter ("A Principal Investigator in Search of a Principal") I also placed it as chapter one in the completed monograph. I felt that I first had to explain—and, in a sense, defend—the ethnographic approach I had pursued. And in a separate article based on that fieldwork, I did the same thing, carefully explaining my fieldwork procedures before introducing any descriptive material (Wolcott, 1974/1987). Today the explication of method that once seemed so critical might be relegated to an appendix in a monograph; for a chapter-length article, a single paragraph may be adequate. My hunch is that if you go on and on about method, whoever is looking over your shoulder (an editor, or a dissertation adviser) will probably ask for less rather than more.

Although it is no longer necessary (or no longer should be necessary) to defend naturalistic or descriptive approaches, or to expound on the advantages and insights to be gained, I do not mean to imply that method simply can be assumed in qualitative study. Readers must be informed about the nature and extent of your data base. When, exactly, did you conduct the fieldwork? How extensive was your involvement (e.g., did you reside at the site or, in contemporary fashion, commute to it, as I have found myself doing in recent years)? To what extent do interviews constitute part of your data base, and what constituted an interview? Are you claiming to triangulate your data? Under what circumstances was information cross-checked, and how are data reported that were not so checked? (Triangulation may sound like a great idea in a research seminar, but wait until your informants find out that you are double-checking everything they tell you! So then, how did you go about confirming information without antagonizing informants?)

Our failure to render full and complete disclosure about our data-gathering procedures gives our methodologically oriented colleagues fits. And rightly so, especially for those among them willing to accept our contributions if we would only provide more careful data about our data. Where and how to include such information is partly a matter of style. The important thing is to be up-front about it, but that is not the same as putting it up front. Regardless of where you review your fieldwork procedures, I think it judicious to examine and (as appropriate) to qualify any and every statement a reader might perceive as a generalization that does not have a corresponding basis in fact. The phrase may get overworked, but scholarship does not suffer when a sentence begins with "As one villager commented . . ." rather than with "Villagers said . . ." For a somewhat idealistic guiding principle, consider Taylor and Bogdan's restatement of this perennial concern: "You should give readers enough information about how the research was conducted to enable them to *discount* your findings" (Taylor and Bogdan, 1984, p. 150; see also Lincoln and Guba's excellent chapter on establishing trustworthiness in qualitative inquiry, 1985, pp. 289-331). Albert Einstein was properly cautious in his purported observation that "no amount of evidence can prove me right, and *any* amount of evidence can prove me wrong" (noted in Miles and Huberman, 1984, p. 242).

Another good starting point is with basic description. What happened? Description is the foundation upon which qualitative research is built. Unless you prove to be a gifted conceptualizer or interpreter, the descriptive account is likely to constitute the most important contribution you have to make. Here you become the storyteller, inviting the reader to see through your eyes what you have seen, then offering your interpretation. Start by presenting a straightforward description of the setting and events. No footnotes, no intrusive analysis—just the facts, carefully presented and interestingly related at an appropriate level of detail.

Vexing questions about the appropriate level of detail in a descriptive narrative have no pat answers. Your purposes in the research are the best guide, although even they may need to be tempered with attention to the art of storytelling. The reactions of outside readers can be helpful once you begin revising your draft. A fieldworker who has been immersed in a research setting may omit details that have become commonplace but are not known to readers unfamiliar with the setting. We also lose track of abbreviations, acronyms, and assumptions that prevail in professional dialogues and regional dialects.

One can argue that until the analysis is well under way it is difficult to know how much to include in the descriptive narrative. I think an equally good case can be made for drafting the descriptive part of the account prior to completing the analysis, and prior even to determining what the course of that analysis will be. Extraneous materials can always be cut; descriptions usually need editing for brevity. Descriptive material written prior to intensive analysis provides a check against the analysis itself: If the facts don't fit, something must be wrong with the interpretation. We may end up with unexplained findings in our work, but we do not fear the unwanted ones that sometimes plague experimental studies.

The question of how to organize a narrative has no pat answers either, although there is an easy fallback resolution. In the absence of a more compelling alternative, relate the story according to either of two chronologies readily at hand: events as they occurred, or events as you learned about and recorded them. Here again, first-person narrative offers an advantage. Although events themselves are ongoing, narrators can introduce characters or settings as first encountered, stopping to fill in with necessary details or letting informants offer different perspectives before continuing with the story.

Whether to weave description and interpretation together or keep them separate—as separate chapters, if one wishes to be dramatic about it—is again a matter of storyteller strategy and personal style. Whatever your decision, do not lose sight of the fact that there is no such thing as pure or natural description. If we were not selective in our focus, we could not produce our accounts: Without some idea of what is to be described, there can be no description. Every step of the way—from setting a problem and selecting an appropriate place, person, or group for studying it; to selective focusing within that setting; to what gets recorded; to which elements of the recorded material make their way into the final account; to the style and authorial voice through which that is accomplished—reflects both conscious and unconscious processes of focus and selection.

You might think of your descriptive sections as subtle analysis, and analytical/interpretive sections as heavy-handed, perhaps even "intrusive" analysis. Qualitative researchers are inclined toward one or the other of these modes. The less theoretically inclined among us stake our reputations on solid ("thick," whatever that is) description, but we also are socialized into the norms of various disciplines. My assessment of qualitative studies in education is that they reveal a tendency toward heavy-handed or intrusive analysis, particularly among educational researchers who feel they not only know their educator audiences but know what is best for them. Informants in their accounts do little talking; the researcher does a lot. Every reported observation or quotation seems to prompt comment or interpretation on the part of the researcher (now turned theorist), something like the chatty guide who becomes rather than gives the tour—and assumes that, without such a monologue, we would not know what to think. I dub studies that exhibit intrusive analysis "Grounded Theory—But Just Barely." A variation of this approach occurs when researchers draw back the curtain to let us watch events unfold but constantly interrupt the account with scholarly interjections, as if duty-bound to remind us of their academic presence.

To be able to meld description and interpretation is a worthy achievement, but at the least suspicion that your analytical asides are interrupting rather than enhancing the narrative, I recommend that you separate the two. You might initially set your interpretive comments in parentheses to determine at a later time whether to leave them where they are, relegate them to footnotes, or collect them under a new heading in which you make a dramatic shift from descriptive to analytical mode.

Meanwhile, start paying close attention to how other researchers handle the interplay between observational data and academic tradition. You may be surprised (even disappointed) to discover that some studies you previously regarded as exemplars of descriptive work actually are constructed upon a conceptual framework, with case data playing only an illustrative role. (Small wonder the data and analysis seemed to join so effortlessly.) This is a different, highly selective way to use qualitative data, something of a complement to the descriptively oriented approach I am describing here. With conceptually oriented studies, a too-leisurely meander through descriptive material can be distracting, just as intrusive analysis can be distracting to a reader expecting a descriptive account. Keep in mind what you have set out to do.

For anyone who follows the recommended strategy to begin with the descriptive account and write the introduction later, let me note as exceptions two short statements that can and should be drafted early, with their location in the completed manuscript to be determined afterward. One is the statement of purpose discussed earlier, a candidate for the opening sentence of any scholarly writing: "The purpose of this study is . . ."

The other is a broad disclaimer in which the researcher makes quite clear his or her recognition of all the limitations of the study (e.g., that it occurred in a particular place, at a particular time, and under particular circumstances; that certain factors render the study atypical; that limited generalization is warranted). This litany of limitations applicable in general to all qualitative research should be coupled with an underscoring of any element deserving of special mention in your particular study. The purpose in putting all this in writing early is that having said it once, you do not have to repeat it every time you introduce a new topic or propose some interpretation. You might think of it as a form of academic throat-clearing, but having stated your disclaimers once and for all you will find it a great relief not to have to begin each sentence with, "Although this is a case study, and limited generalization is warranted . . ."

The Problem of Focus

I keep returning to the importance of the critical sentence, "The purpose of this study is . . ." But what if you can't complete that sentence, because that happens to be the very point on which you are stuck?

If that is where you are stuck, writing is not your problem. Your problem is conceptual, one that my colleague and mentor George Spindler refers to as "the problem problem." If you don't feel you can make adequate headway with your problem problem by just staring into space, you might try one of two approaches.

One way to overcome the problem problem is to invite a colleague with a good analytical turn of mind to have lunch with you. Order lightly so you can dominate the conversation, chatting about your research. Solicit help with your problem of focus. Your colleague may not prove as helpful as you hoped, but giving words to unexpressed thoughts may help you. When other people with other thoughts on their minds offer feedback, even if it widely misses the mark, you may discover that you are closer than you realized to pinpointing your own ideas. Do consider a wider network of colleagues, however, than may first come to mind. Graduate students can be a great sounding board, not only for fellow students but for professors; similarly, professors can be helpful to students, including students who are not their advisees. But I'm serious about lunch, in the sense of getting away from interruption and from locales where status is fixed. What I tell students in my office always sounds a bit stilted; over lunch, my ideas have to fend for themselves (as well as compete with the French fries).

The other alternative—and you might want to use both—is to reinterpret writing as a way to *resolve* your problem problem rather than as the source of it. With only yourself in mind as audience, try the freewriting mentioned earlier. Think on paper. Try to pin down your thoughts by giving them what Becker (1986, p. 56) calls "physical embodiment." You may discover that a scholarly explication of the problem is warranted prior to proposing new empirical research. Possibly you can develop a stimulating article (or organize a good symposium) because the problem itself has never been set carefully.

I am attracted by the idea—new to me—of thinking about research as problem setting, rather than problem solving. In much of the applied educational research that I see, the outcomes do not set well because the problems addressed are not well set. In this regard we veterans miss opportunities to model good research practice for our graduate students. New enthusiasm for qualitative approaches, especially as it has come to mean and invite more open-endedness in what we look for and how we proceed, has exacerbated the problem of problem setting (also referred to as problem finding or problem posing; see Wolcott, 1988). It makes no sense to go off conducting research without an idea of what is to be researched: empty-headedness is not the same as open-mindedness. Problem setting is a scholarly activity reflected in the qualitative research that follows from it, for better or for worse.

My bias may be showing, but it has always seemed to me that anthropologically oriented ethnographers have it easier than other qualitative researchers in this regard because they have a broadly stated mandate always before them. They study culture in general, certain aspects of it in particular: world view, cultural themes, culture change and adaptation, social structure. Elsewhere I have discussed this as "ethnographic intent," arguing that purpose rather than method lies at the heart of ethnography (Wolcott, 1987, 1990a). In some quarters, qualitative research—even ethnography itself—has become synonymous with "going to have a look around." No wonder inexperienced researchers have trouble writing up their studies when they set out with objectives defined so loosely or settings mistaken for problems.

At the same time, I do not wish to create an impression that a research focus is a sacred thing—that once declared it deserves unwavering loyalty or that, once fixed, the course of a research project must never be altered. Part of the strategy of qualitative inquiry (a key advantage of the flexibility we claim for it) is that our research questions themselves remain under continual scrutiny. Nothing should prevent a research question or problem statement from undergoing the same metamorphosis as the researcher during the course of a study. Data gathering and data analysis inform the problem statement, just as the statement informs the data gathering. Proposals are just that: proposals, beginnings, starting places, literal points of departure. We are burdened with strictures that we ourselves have built into our expectations about the proper conditions of research. A statement attributed to biologist Paul Weiss helps me maintain perspective in these matters: "Nobody who followed the scientific method ever discovered anything interesting" (quoted in Keesing and Keesing, 1971, p. 10).

Problems of Sorting and Organizing Data

If your data remain in essentially the same form in which you originally collected them—pages and pages of notes and interview protocols—I hope you don't advertise to colleagues that you have "writer's block." Your blockage has occurred at a prior stage. If you have embarked on a descriptive broadside, you had better get back to some very basic sorting into some very basic categories, and then see if you can discern some very basic questions that could guide the development of your account.

Some questions that guide me (but may not work as well for you) are: What is going on here? What do people in this setting have to know (individually or collectively) in order to do what they are doing? How are skills and attitudes transmitted and acquired, particularly in the absence of intentional efforts at instruction? Such questions guide my research and my thinking about culture acquisition, the underlying concern in my present work. I do not have a problem with focus. Any problem I have is with people who neither share my sense of excitement that these are wonderful questions nor have equally wonderful (to them, at least) questions of their own to propose. What are the questions that guide you, either of the intermediate range that guide current work, or the overarching type that shape entire careers?

When you are ready to do some initial sorting of data, begin by identifying the broadest categories imaginable. How about place and/or time and/or actors as a start? You might consider introducing your study with a static picture in which you set the scene and introduce major actors one at a time, much as if you were writing a play. Continue presenting these "still shots" until you have enough elements on hand (or actors figuratively on stage) to set things in motion. This is how George Foster (1969) went about examining processes in applied anthropology. He first looked at what he called the *target group,* the people targeted for change. Next, he did a predictable anthropological turnabout and directed attention to the *innovating organization* or donor group, the so-called agents of change. What was it they wanted—for the target group and, as well, for themselves? Having examined the two groups separately, he then turned attention to the arenas in which they interacted.

Foster's approach offers a straightforward way to organize a study of directed change—and an awful lot (both literally and figuratively!) of dissertation studies are focused on that topic, although they typically lack adequate attention to the full context of change. In terms of sorting, one could start with the same categories Foster identified: target group, innovating organization, and interaction setting (Foster, 1969, chapters 4, 5, and 6, respectively). Foster's categories not only provide an excellent way to organize a study of change processes, they provide a model for organizing virtually any field study focused on the effects some group wants to produce in another.

Begin sorting by finding a few categories sufficiently comprehensive to allow you to sort *all* your data. Remember that you are only sorting. If you are having problems with what ought to be a straightforward task, you are probably starting to develop theory, regardless of how modest. You are trying to take two steps at once. Try one at a time!

I first encountered this problem years ago when I began to organize the material from my huge (in terms of data gathered) ethnography of a school principal. I kept adding more and more categories, and the sorting became more and more complex. I had the good luck to meet Howard Becker at the time, and he suggested that if I was having trouble sorting things out, I must be doing more than sorting things out. Once I simplified the system, the sorting was easy; then I began making refinements.

Becker's advice in those pre-processor days was to put important bits of data (quotes from an informant, an observation, a vignette, an insight recorded during notetaking) on individual 3 × 5 or 5 × 8 cards, or half-sheets of typing paper. The sorting was literal: You sat at a table (or on the floor) and physically divided up your great bundle of data "cards" by putting them into smaller piles according to categories that allowed you a first run at organizing your material. The big technological breakthrough of the day was the key-sort punch card, an index card ringed with holes on all sides that could be punched open according to whatever coding system the researcher devised. With your cards lined up in front of you, each containing some discrete bit of data and code-punched around the edges, you had only to insert one or more rods through the stack of cards and then shake them. Your coding and punching system enabled the rods to separate the cards you wanted from the others. (For current practice on coding and analysis, see Becker, 1986, pp. 59ff; Bernard, 1988, especially chapters 14 and 15.)

Some researchers continue to use coding systems based on that punch-card principle. I don't, because when I might have used them I couldn't afford them, and I grew accustomed to putting data on 5 × 8 papers easily typed or handwritten, easily stored, and easily sorted. My little stacks of cards or papers may seem archaic in a computer age, but I describe them to help others visualize processes partially hidden by modern technology. I marvel at software programs like THE ETHNOGRAPH, QUALPRO, or TEXT ANALYSIS PACKAGE (TAP) designed for data management with personal computers (see Conrad and Reinharz, 1984; Heise, 1981; Pfaffenberger, 1988; Seidel and Clark, 1984; see also a brief review in *American Anthropologist*, 1989, pp. 1055-1056, of a software and "shareware" program, ANTHROPAC, developed by Stephen Borgatti specifically for managing and analyzing fieldwork data). Keep in mind, however, that most programs are attuned better to the almost limitless capacities of microcomputers than to the finite capacities of human researchers. In THE ETHNOGRAPH, for example, a "line" of text—ranging from a single word to an entire interview—can be coded into as many as seven different categories. This is a great convenience once one has arrived at the categorizing stage. But for anyone having trouble *sorting* data, a program that allowed initially for no more than two or three categories might prove a blessing rather than a needless constraint.

I repeat: The critical task in qualitative research is not to accumulate all the data you can, but to "can" (i.e., get rid of) most of the data you accumulate. This requires constant winnowing. The trick is to discover essences and then to reveal those essences with sufficient context, yet not become mired trying to include everything that might possibly be described. Audiotapes, videotapes, and now computer capabilities entreat us to do just the opposite; they have gargantuan appetites *and* stomachs. Because we can accommodate ever-increasing quantities of data—mountains of it—we have to be careful not to get buried by avalanches of our own making.

This problem of data overload has a parallel in one of the unanticipated consequences of the copy machines now so readily available in our libraries. In my student days, when we were given reading assignments, we went to the library and read the material, typically distilling the key ideas and copying a few telling quotes onto reading cards. Today's students copy entire articles and books intact. Their visits to the library are more efficient than ours were, except in one important way: When they leave, they have not begun the assignment. When they do get around to their reading, they probably will underline or highlight huge passages of text with a felt pen, rather than identify key phrases and summarize the rest in their own words. This is not good training for descriptive research. The parallel style in fieldwork is referred to disparagingly as the vacuum-cleaner approach, in which fieldworkers attempt to see and record *everything*. There is a division between those qualitative researchers who want to impress upon students how *much* they can observe and those who place the emphasis on how *well*.

Let me bring this message home with the consequences of the vacuum-cleaner approach for a dissertation study that is being written—or, more truthfully, not being written—even as I compose these sentences. I am a member of the dissertation committee, not the chairperson, but in some ways I feel responsible as the instructor who "inspired" a capable doctoral student to use a qualitative approach on the basis of course work taken with me in anthropology and education. The student, Alfred (a pseudonym, of course), is a veteran public-school teacher with a particular interest in social studies. Alfred originally proposed an ambitious year-long study of his own social studies classroom, including videotaping, diary-keeping, test results, student reactions, observations conducted by independent observers—you name it, he included it. As committee members, we were remiss (I now realize) in not pressing for sharper focus at the time of the proposal review, but we did not want to appear carping and we lauded Alfred's thoroughness and capability for hard work. Also, we had at hand his massive review of the literature, which we mistakenly took as a good sign instead of a bad one, for it was exhaustive rather than selective.

We haven't seen Alfred on campus for a couple of years. He has returned to classroom teaching, having used his allotted study leave to pursue course work *prior* to dissertation research rather than after it, in the typical but unfortunate pattern of doctoral programs in professional schools. We keep hearing that the first three chapters are ready; this isn't much of a progress report, however. The proposal was so extensive it virtually overwhelmed chapter one. The literature review constituted a ready-made, if tedious, chapter two. Now, chapter three exhausts method.

There is every professional and personal reason in the world for Alfred to finish his study, and perhaps he will. I can only surmise at this point that he genuinely is stuck, so mired down in data after so long a time that he has become immobilized. He's too proud to seek help, presumably interpreting his problem as a personal failure rather than recognizing the inherent trap in the boundless freedom of an inadequately focused descriptive study. The face-saving element in all this is that Alfred's problem has been attributed to writer's block. The cold hard fact is that he doesn't know what to say and what not to say; he is still hoping to include everything.

3. KEEPING GOING

Once your writing is under way, I assume that if you have something to say and a plan for saying it, you can progress satisfactorily on your own. Not only would you be better off left alone, I doubt that you would take time to read something like this, for it is addressed to a problem you do not have. Further, not only all writers but each individual piece of writing takes on a personality and direction of its own. The best advice I have for any writer already writing is conveyed in my chapter titles: Once you get going, keep going.

I do know that in addition to being an act of arrogance, writing is also a splendid test of one's tolerance for deferred gratification. Even when the writing seems to be going well, there could hardly be gratification enough to warrant the time and commitment necessary to keep on keeping on. You have to work without feedback or encouragement. Your only measure of progress may be the diminishing number of topics still to be addressed and a slowly mounting set of pages of uneven quality that may fall far short of original hopes and expectations.

Rely on grim determination and keep plugging away. I can suggest a few pointers that you may take as advice from an old hand, but the issues raised are more important than the resolutions I can propose. Anything goes that results in a tangible written product moving you toward a satisfactory final manuscript and that offers a toehold for subsequent revision. For analogy let me suggest the criterion used by most of my Chinese acquaintances around the world whenever I ask if I am using chopsticks the proper way: "Harry, is the food getting to your mouth?"

In writing, results are what count; the end justifies the means. How much coffee you drink, sleep you lose, days you "waste," even how awful your first drafts look—none of these really matter. Be ever mindful of Becker's wise counsel that "the only version that counts is the last one" (1986, p. 21).

Stay With It

If you have engaged in substantial fieldwork, be prepared to spend from several months to a year completing your writing. Rosalie Wax's sage advice is to allow as much time for analysis and writing as time spent in the field—and, as she adds, even more if you are "really astute and can get away with it" (Wax, 1971, p. 45). From the outset, pace yourself for an activity in which it is critical to sustain interest, not merely to capture an occasional burst of energy of the sort that once got you through school assignments (graduate studies included). "The precondition for writing well," Peter Elbow observes, "is being able to write badly and to write when you are not in the mood" (1981, p. 373). Set reasonable expectations and make a firm commitment that writing time will receive top priority. Be demanding of yourself. Authors who make a living at it attend to their writing not only on a daily basis but for a seven- rather than a five-day week.

At the same time, do recognize that writing up a study entails related processes described in the previous chapter, as well as new ones that accompany the creation of a manuscript: rereading, resorting, refining, rechecking, revising, and time for just staring into space (ruminating, if you're addicted to alliteration). Friends who look for encouraging roles don't necessarily confer a favor by asking, "Well, how many pages today?" Maybe you can cool them out with a reminder that writing qualitative studies entails more than putting words on paper, but my guess is that you have to convince yourself of that as well.

The "Expanding Drop File" Approach

Some years ago I was a consultant to a field-based study of educational change in which a number of qualitatively oriented researchers—with backgrounds in anthropology, sociology, and educational research—were conducting long-term studies in 10 rural communities throughout the United States. A major responsibility at each site was for these resident researchers (on-site researchers, or OSRs, as they came to be known in project lingo) to develop a monograph describing the community, the schools, and the nature and consequences of the requisite effort at educational change.

Project directors were concerned, with good cause as it turned out, that not every on-site researcher would actually complete a monograph. I was asked to suggest ways that might foster success without infringing unnecessarily on the independent spirit and effort of each fieldworker. The directors recognized as well that preparation of the case studies had to compete with numerous other responsibilities imposed on the researchers, such as gathering survey data for a cross-site study and continuing the fieldwork throughout the duration of the project. Nor did they want to impose a rigid schedule of deadlines that required everyone to submit manuscripts in lockstep fashion on an identical outline of topics.

As the directors correctly anticipated (and feared), not every fieldworker completed the writing project. You cannot *make* people write. You can tie remuneration to receipt of a completed report in contract research, but given the long duration of the project these researchers were on annual salaries. To threaten to withhold payment pending submission of a case study was tantamount to dismissing them as regular employees. Those experiencing difficulty drafting their case studies might have seized the opportunity to escape from what was looming as an onerous professional obligation.

I suggested that each on-site researcher begin by proposing a table of contents for the monograph projected for that site. (Does this surprise you?) A collective review of all proposed tables of contents for the 10 sites would constitute the agenda for a major project seminar. At that seminar, researchers would elaborate on and defend their ideas, and project coordinators would suggest (or impose) any standardization of format necessary for the project as a whole. True, this might have precipitated a moment for critical and delicate negotiation, but the research organization did have contractual obligations to meet in addition to its genuine efforts to treat the fieldworkers as qualified professionals. Following that negotiated agreement, the preparation of individual monographs would begin.

I proposed that each fieldworker prepare a drop file, with each separate folder within it devoted to one of the chapters identified in the proposed (and now formally approved) table of contents. Each folder, in turn, was to go through a roughly comparable sequence of development—beginning with brief memos or jottings or a set of data cards; progressing either to a tight outline for the chapter or a rough first draft; and thence, through multiple revisions as necessary, to a completed draft of a chapter ready for inclusion in the gradually evolving monograph. The problem of employee accountability, under circumstances that I dubbed "contract anthropology" (Wolcott, 1975, p. 110; see also Clinton, 1975, 1976; Fitzsimmons, 1975), was revealed in such "hypothetical" questions posed at headquarters as "How do we know whether the fieldworker is really at the site?" or "How do we know whether progress is being made on the monograph?" These pervasive concerns could be alleviated simply by asking each fieldworker to forward evidence of progress in any one file at each regular reporting period. Meanwhile, fieldworkers would have considerable latitude from one reporting period to the next in deciding whether to devote their current effort to preparing outlines for proposed chapters, writing first drafts of new chapters, or revising and refining chapter manuscripts as the projected monograph began to take shape.

Built into my production scheme was a recognition that no two researchers were likely to be, or needed to be, working on the same topic or at the same speed. It also allowed for periods when formal productivity might be low—for example, when the researchers' efforts toward the site case study were sidetracked by project-wide assignments, or by attendance at professional meetings when they periodically reported to audiences of peers and patrons.

Although the procedure I proposed was not formally adopted within the project, I think it eminently workable, potentially as useful for the lone researcher as for someone coordinating a large-scale project involving parallel studies at multiple sites. (Procedures for cross-site analysis receive major attention in Miles and Huberman's *Qualitative Data Analysis,* 1984, but that gets into issues of synthesizing and aggregating cases; see also Noblit and Hare, 1988.) The critical problem is to ensure that one's work moves forward, however slowly, rather than to allow it ever to come to a stop.

In addition to major chapters reserved for description and interpretation, one's own expanding drop file—real or imagined—ought to contain some potentially modest assignments such as drafting acknowledgments or organizing references, in addition to longer but nonetheless doable assignments such as writing the method chapter (or, as discussed previously, the method appendix). The total "file" of written products emanating from a project might also include symposia or seminar papers and articles intended for journal publication.

A major writing project such as a monograph or dissertation does not proceed with every section at the same stage of development. The more ambitious the total project, the more advantageous to have different parts at different stages of development, so that chores can be varied, time and mood accommodated. Unforeseen delays should never bring the research and writing to a complete halt. Anticipate (and expect) delay and have other tasks in mind to which you can turn, perhaps including the preparation of the first draft of your next article, proposal, or project.

In my own writing, preparing the first draft is the most difficult step; revising and editing are more satisfying. No question that revising and editing are critical tasks, and for some the hardest, but I do not concur with Peter Elbow (1981, p. 21) that they are also the most unpleasant, except when I must make major cuts—a topic for the next chapter. For me, writing enervates and editing exhilarates. Sometimes the writing goes excruciatingly slowly. On days when it doesn't seem to be going at all, you can devote a few moments to bringing the references section up-to-date, so that you are armed with a ready reply should some insensitive but well-meaning colleague raise the anxiety-provoking question: "How many pages this week?"

A suggestion that experienced writers offer for helping to regain momentum when you return to your writing is to give special attention to the point at which you quit each day. The idea is to stop where you can easily take up again. At the least, jot some key words that capture your train of thought. If you are in the middle of a paragraph that you know you can finish, stop there. If you are copying a long quote from an academic source or an informant, stop at the beginning rather than at the end, so that you can get right to work at the next writing opportunity.

I admit that I often begin my day's writing by reviewing and editing what I wrote or reviewed the day before, a slow way to get a fast start. You must see through that approach, for I have confessed that I find editing more enjoyable than writing. Editing obviously can become an escape from writing, or at least a hindrance to getting through a first draft. Nevertheless, looking back over yesterday's work does offer a way to get warmed up on days when the sentences do not flow. Having struggled with particular words or ideas on the previous occasion, I sometimes see a better resolution at my next try. The editing-reviewing may take up to an hour—about one quarter of the minimum time I try to set aside for writing. It also violates my puritan ethic, which holds that the pleasure should come after the pain, not before. But it is a concession I make in order to accomplish my major objective: to keep at it, once the writing begins. Make some measurable progress in the development of your manuscript every writing day.

When It's Time for Details, Get Them Right the First Time

The proper form for citations, references, footnotes, margin headings, and so forth required by your discipline, your institution (if writing a dissertation), or your intended journal or publisher ought to be clearly in mind as you work. Your default mode should be the accepted standard for your discipline, with which you ought to be completely familiar. When preparing material in an unfamiliar format, keep a recent issue of a professional journal or an authoritative style manual at hand.

Of course, you may not want to be bothered with such detail in early drafts, unless you are that bleeder type who wants everything correct from the outset. At whatever point you do attend to details, do so carefully, correctly, and in proper final form. Double-check against the original source and be done with it. I recommend that you record full citations and accurate quotations in the first draft [or flag things that need to be checked with brackets and a note to yourself, like this]. The more details you can handle routinely, the more efficient your work. It is not only efficiency that you gain: You also free yourself from having to attend to picayune details during final revision when your attention should be on whether you have your own words right, not worrying about someone else's.

Are you aware of the variation in the spellings offered in different dictionaries, the citation forms preferred in different fields (as well as preferences from one journal to the next in the same field), and the form and placement of footnotes or endnotes? If you have never published a book, you may not realize that copy editors develop an individual style sheet for each manuscript. A style sheet is a record of the decisions about spellings, hyphens, headings and subheadings, footnotes, or anything else about your manuscript that needs to be noted, so that usages *within your text* are consistent.

It's not a bad idea to develop a style sheet of your own special and frequently used words as you become aware of them (e.g., *adviser* or *advisor;* gaining *entry* or *entrée; judgment* or *judgement; macroculture* or *macro-culture:* which form are you going to use?) so that you use them consistently. As you become ever more conscious about word choice, you may also want to keep track of words new to you that you'd like to slip in at first opportunity, just as you may have identified utterly awesome ones you've personally earmarked for extinction. Style sheets reflect preferences and customary usages; be prepared to capitulate if you find yourself at odds with editorial policy, but raise a question before you do, because styles are always in flux. Publishers' style sheets and the major style manuals undergo continual revision; the influential *Chicago Manual of Style* is presently in its thirteenth.

Follow a consistent style for making your own permanent bibliographic references. Do not hesitate to record more information than ordinarily required by abbreviated formats: full and complete titles; full names of all authors; full journal names, with volume and issue number; inclusive page numbers for articles and for chapters in edited volumes; publisher and place of publication; and date of publication. When citing material published long ago but available to you only in a newer edition, record the date of original publication as well as the date of the edition you have cited, and include both dates in your in-text citations (e.g., "Malinowski (1922/1984)"). I also try to track sources *forward* by including both in my own notes and in formal citations any available information about materials republished or reissued. This practice is especially helpful for references to journal articles subsequently reprinted in books, or to formerly out-of-print sources that again become available, as with many of the case studies in cultural anthropology originally published in the 1960s and 1970s. Not all of this information is required by every field, journal, or publishing house. Yet it takes only a moment to make a complete record in your original entry, and it can save time if you later discover, for example, that a journal to which you have submitted your article uses authors' full names rather than only first initials.

One further suggestion about academic references: Make your citations as explicit as possible. There are occasions when global reference to an entire book is appropriate, but if you take critical note of the way academic writers employ references, you will catch many of them playing a great name-dropping game. They lob references like so many snowballs over a fence, an indiscriminate barrage that fails to achieve the kind of specificity appropriate in scholarly writing. To be really helpful, go beyond minimum expectations (author, date, page reference) to inform your readers of the nature of the material to which you make reference and, unless it is apparent in your text, your reason for citing it (i.e., whether it is your source, a source of further information, or a source for comparison or contrast [cf.]). Most readers will not consult your sources; they count on you to inform them. This is one reason for being accurate and complete. Conversely, some readers *will* consult your citations; that is another reason.

Getting Feedback

The compound word "feedback" contains two elements. The first implies nurturance; most authors crave it. The second indicates direction: backward. Feedback draws attention to the already done, rather than the yet-to-do. Keep that in mind when you begin wishing for it. Don't seek it too soon, especially if it might divert attention from completing the full draft by tempting you to start revising what you have already written. I recognize the good intentions of professors who want to approve (which, unfortunately, may also mean disapprove) the first three chapters of their students' dissertations, but the advice I give my doctoral students is the same I give other writers: Work on your own as long as possible before inviting feedback. When you are ready, seek it judiciously. A little goes a long way.

Timely and useful feedback on writing is hard to give and hard to take. The problem is compounded in qualitative research because there are so many dimensions on which feedback can be offered: whether one has identified the right story to tell, how well it has been told, and how well it has been analyzed and interpreted. And as with any writing, it is easier to identify problems, difficult sentences, and alternative explanations than to know what to say about particularly well-conceived studies, particularly well-turned phrases, or particularly insightful interpretations, other than a clichéd "I really liked this" or "Great!" Even gentle reviewer-critics are more likely to fault weaknesses in a manuscript than to applaud strengths, unless they render only a global reaction and leave the nitty-gritty to others. Thus, regardless of intent, feedback tends to be disproportionately critical and negative. Your only consolation may be that the more painstaking the critique, the more you may assume that your critic has taken your effort seriously.

Select early readers with care and instruct them as to the kind (and extent) of criticism you believe will be helpful. I prefer to invite friends and/or fellow authors to be my earliest reviewers. My assumption is that they constitute a support group who will attend to finding ways to help me say what I am trying to say in particular instances, rather than dwell on my (or my manuscript's) apparently not-yet-attained potential.

Yet I value any feedback I receive short of flat-out rejection. I would not think of formally submitting a manuscript that had not been given a critical once-over by colleagues, both as it was being developed and in almost-final form. I say "almost-final" because as long as we invite critique, we will get it: The process never ends. If you insist on someone offering final approval, you will have to be candid in soliciting it.

In seeking feedback, keep in mind a distinction between the conduct of research and the reporting of research. Research purposes come first. Eloquence can enhance a good study but it cannot save a poor one. Early readers should be directed to look primarily at the accuracy and adequacy of detail, at how the problem is stated and the account unfolds, and at the appropriateness of the interpretation. Outside readers may recognize elements to which a preoccupied researcher has become oblivious. There may be little point in worrying about the niceties of style if the content is not well in place, if interpretation misses the mark, if the focus is misplaced, or if the account lacks balance. But recognize as well that reviewers are not likely to have something to contribute to every aspect. Steel yourself for the likelihood that, regardless of how you instruct them, your critics probably will say more about style than content. It is, after all, *your* account; others will see their role as helping you to convey your ideas, not to counter with their own.

An ideal combination of early reviewers might include a colleague from one's academic field to attend to framework and analysis, and a reader familiar with the research setting to read for accuracy, completeness, and sensitivity to the people being described. Like many fieldworkers, I make an effort to have readers in the setting look at developing drafts (especially the descriptive sections). I regard this as an integral element of fieldwork, often noting in subsequent drafts the reactions and comments prompted by earlier readings. (For the pros and cons of this practice, see Emerson and Pollner, 1988.)

Bearing in mind that today's informants and collaborators not only expect but sometimes insist on reading our drafts prior to general circulation, it is also advisable to anticipate how disagreements are to be negotiated. My policy is to share a prerelease draft with interested informants and to take into account any reservations expressed. I believe that a researcher is ill advised, however, to offer full veto power—even to key informants—lest the project remain in jeopardy throughout its entire duration. Researchers, too, are human subjects who need protection from unnecessary risk.

Nonetheless, I delay sharing a developing manuscript with *anyone* for as long as possible. I want to be sure I've said what I want to say, and said it well enough that my ideas are clearly stated, before subjecting my words to the scrutiny of others. During the year I devoted to writing my doctoral dissertation, following a year of fieldwork, I made only brief visits to the university campus. I did not need the company of other anxious dissertation writers to get my own writing done. I had a story to tell, and I needed to tell it my way first. I sought little advice from my dissertation committee prior to submitting a completed draft. Had it proved unacceptable, I was prepared to undertake any necessary rewriting, but not until I had rendered my own account.

On the other hand, I eagerly anticipated long work sessions with my fellow graduate student Ron Rohner and his wife Evelyn. We met regularly to discuss our progress, exchange information, and share and critique early drafts. Our independent but somewhat complementary studies were based on anthropologically oriented fieldwork conducted at the same time, in neighboring villages among the same people, and under the same mentor (Rohner and Rohner, 1970/1986; Wolcott, 1967/1989). Like the fieldwork on which it was based, our writing proceeded in a climate of mutual help and encouragement.

When time is of the essence, or you find yourself unduly concerned about how the writing is going, I recommend finding some patient soul (for that reason alone this probably will not be an academic colleague) who will read and provide intentionally encouraging feedback. Even better, ask someone to read your words aloud to you without comment, or with only general and supportive suggestions such as "That reads well" or "This needs more explanation." Hearing your words read aloud can help you concentrate on what actually has reached paper—the experience as you are creating it for others, out of your experience. They are not the same.

We do not recognize the rhythms and patterns of our own speech. What we write usually reads well to us (i.e., literally "sounds right") because we know how to read it. But no two humans share identical language patterns. When that oral reader stumbles—or not-so-subtly gasps for air, as my friend Anna Kohner used to do while reading aloud long sentences of early drafts of my dissertation—the author needs to get busy with the editing pencil.

Some Specific Suggestions To Keep You Going

Let me conclude by reiterating the central idea of this chapter: Keep the writing moving forward. Get the essence of your study committed to paper, no matter how rough or incomplete it may seem. Do not lose sight of the fact that well-focused interpretive statements may help you improve the problem statement, just as your developing analysis may help you make better decisions about the descriptive material, although the descriptive material will probably (but not necessarily) precede it in the completed manuscript. Further thoughts:

- Keep your focus in mind as you weave the story and offer your interpretation, but maintain a healthy skepticism about the focus itself. Always consider the possibility that you are not yet on the mark. A guiding question: "What is this (really) a study of?"
- Your major concern, especially in writing the first draft, is to get rid of data—to focus progressively, to home in on your topic. You can note in passing (in literal notes to yourself, or in asides shared with readers) important and intriguing issues you must leave for another time.
- Do not allow yourself to get stuck because of data you do not have, or problems and elements that you do not understand or feel you cannot (and perhaps will never be able to) interpret adequately. Note whatever is bothering you, either for yourself, if you think things can be remedied, or for your reader, if the problem seems likely to remain fixed at that stage. Then get on with it. Readers will not be offended if you do not claim to know everything.

- Unless absolutely forbidden to do so by a stuffy editor or dissertation committee, write in the first person. Put yourself squarely in the scene, but don't take center stage. The world does not need more sentences of the sort that begin, "It appears to this writer . . ." or "What is being said here is . . ."
- Try writing your descriptive passages entirely in the past tense if you find yourself constantly moving between present and past. Admittedly, the past tense seems to "kill off" everyone as soon as an action is completed. It also does strange things to alive-and-well informants, particularly if you begin writing while still conducting fieldwork. By the time your manuscript has gone through many iterations, editorial review, and publication you will discover that the past tense no longer seems so strange, and you will not have left informants forever doing and saying whatever they happened to be doing and saying during your brief tenure.
- Use your extensive field notes and fieldwork experience to provide concrete illustrations and examples. Never underestimate the power of specific instances to support your generalizations and to inform and reach out to your reader, what Geertz eloquently describes as "the power of the scientific imagination to bring us into touch with the lives of strangers" (1973, p. 16).
- Write for your peers. Pitch the level of discussion to an audience of readers who do *not* know what you are talking about. Write your dissertation with fellow graduate students in mind, not your learned committee members. Address your subsequent studies to the many who do not know, not the few who do.
- Heed the admonitions so frequently given in the interest of improving prose. Try to avoid wordiness, passive or convoluted constructions, long words and pompous phrases, abstract nouns and faulty pronoun references, misplaced modifiers, and nonparallel constructions. But never allow such admonitions to hinder initial efforts to get ideas written down; you can attend to style and correctness in the later stages of revising and editing, and you can get help from others with those aspects of writing. No one need ever see your early drafts. As your ideas take shape and become more elegant, take pleasure in crafting sentences worthy of them.

4. TIGHTENING UP

Some of the best advice I've ever seen for writers happened to be included with the directions I found for assembling a new wheelbarrow: *Make sure all parts are properly in place before tightening.*

To press the analogy a bit further, fieldwork and data sorting in qualitative research might be likened to collecting and identifying the parts of a wheelbarrow. Then you need a workable sequence for joining the parts. Before you start tightening, take a look at how the whole thing is coming together. Do you have everything you need? (And, do you need everything you have? Remember, you're only supposed to be tightening up that wheelbarrow, not filling it!)

Whether writing up your research entails a project report, a journal article, a dissertation, a technically oriented monograph, or a book, my guess is that as the material takes shape you will worry that the descriptive account is too long, the interpretation or analysis lacks the power you hoped to achieve, and you cannot figure out what to say in conclusion. Dismaying as these problems may appear, you are making headway if they are yours. Think how much better off you are than a researcher who discovers that the data are thin, or the analysis and conclusions unwarranted.

No amount of fancy editing can transform an inadequate data base into a solid piece of research—although candor on the part of the researcher may preserve ideas, insights, and questions that have merit independent of fizzled fieldwork. Don't fool yourself for a moment that some fancy combination of boldface type, shadow letters, underlined words, or whatever format or lettering tricks you can do with word processing or laser printing can improve anything except the looks of a manuscript. (Fancy title pages on term papers always arouse my suspicion.) Qualitative studies are dependent on how they read, not how they look. Fieldwork may be the dramatic part, but the quality of the desk work holds the real key. Writing is integral to qualitative inquiry, not an adjunct. Some researchers may achieve brilliant results through seemingly effortless prowess with prose, but what most of us accomplish is achieved through sustained effort at editing and revision. These are the processes discussed here.

Reviewing for Content and Style

If I have given the impression that I take style to be more important than content, let me now correct that impression. Content is paramount—*what* you have to say, not how you say it. Style is critical but auxiliary in reporting qualitative research, necessary but not sufficient. An attractive feature about style is that it is amenable to discussions like this. No one can teach you how to write; lots of people can help you write a bit better.

I have never met anyone who reads qualitative studies for their style. What Geertz says of anthropological writing applies to qualitative research in general: "Good anthropological texts are plain texts, unpretending. They neither invite literary-critical close reading nor reward it" (1988, p. 2). For the most part, however, our efforts are focused on other humans working through their own everyday lives, and our studies ought to be not only unpretentious but intriguing as well. When they are not, when our accounts appear sterile and lifeless, how often is inattention to writing at fault? Our peculiar genius often seems to take the life out of our cases rather than celebrate the life in them. Our opportunity is also our challenge: to portray real people doing and saying real things, seen through the eyes of another human observer.

With a completed draft of the full account in hand—including initial attempts at analysis or interpretation, no matter how rudimentary—the process of tightening begins in earnest. Tightening is the part of the writing process that I most enjoy, although I do not suggest that working through successive drafts of a manuscript is without agonies of its own. I try to express thoughts clearly the first time; I do not write poorly in order to make revision challenging. I take little delight in recognizing long, unnecessarily complex, and poorly formed sentences or paragraphs that I thought were OK when I wrote them. Worse yet, behind many such sentences lurks a poorly formed idea. I often wonder if my thinking is as convoluted as my writing. (If so, is the problem diminishing with experience or getting worse with age?) Thoughts seemingly satisfactory in the abstract seldom appear with comparable clarity when written.

With an entire manuscript drafted, one also realizes that it is no small trick to get description and interpretation to match. We carry in our heads far more of our studies than we ever commit to print, a fact always more apparent in reading the work of others than our own. One sometimes wonders whether researchers pay sufficient attention to what they actually have written. Is the narrative account sufficient to support the analysis? The resolution lies not in faulting the analysis, but in keeping in mind that analysis helps to form the descriptive account, just as the descriptive account provides the substance for analysis. I have suggested that writing the narrative description is a good place to begin, but this does not mean the descriptive account then becomes sacrosanct. Until a manuscript is in print, not a word in it is sacrosanct. (You cannot be that cavalier with material quoted from your sources, of course, but the choice and extent of such quotations remains yours and yours alone.)

As the analysis takes shape, some material originally included may become superfluous, just as other sections may need to be fleshed out with more detail. Anthropologist Michael Agar (1980) offers this description of the process:

> You learn something ("collect some data"), then you try to make sense out of it ("analysis"), then you go back and see if the interpretation makes sense in light of new experience ("collect more data"), then you refine your interpretation ("more analysis"), and so on. The process is dialectic, not linear. (p. 9)

The nexus between description and analysis in the written account is also dialectic—each process informing the other, each helping with the important work of reducing the detail, maintaining the focus, and moving ahead with the story. Where your descriptive account is "thin" because your data are thin, you are well advised to exhibit both honesty and restraint. There is nothing wrong with sharing hunches or impressions, provided they are labeled as such. Nor can you be faulted for pointing to the kind of data that would be necessary to support a generalization you *believe* to be warranted but are not actually prepared to make.

The tightening phase is also the time to begin looking for needless repetition. Because our studies sometimes take years to research and months to write, we forget that they are read in a matter of hours, even minutes. Sentences written weeks apart and revised days apart may be read moments apart. Astute collegial reviewers can identify repetitions that we ourselves no longer recognize. How surprising to find a comment penned by a colleague, "Didn't you just say all this about three pages back?" But how much better such gentle admonition from a friend than to find a terse comment from an anonymous reviewer: "Redundant. Needs rewriting."

Revising Versus Editing

Writers writing self-consciously about writing sometimes distinguish between revising and editing, the former in reference to reviewing content, the latter regarding style, correctness, and other details. The distinction correctly sets priorities: Content comes first. But I think it also fosters a mistaken image of a two-step process. Editing presupposes something to edit, and that something is the heart of it, not simply a first step. At the same time, the implication that everything I write requires revision is a little harsh on my author-ego, even if it may be essentially correct. I find myself referring to manuscripts as revised *after* I revise them, but while actually engaging in the process I prefer to think (and announce) that I am editing, regardless of whether I am performing a major overhaul or minor tuning. I admit to revising only when I must change a format, make cuts or revisions called for by an editor, or undertake a substantial rewrite, such as "dedissertationizing" my doctoral research for publication (Wolcott, 1967/1989). Most of what I call editing would probably be called revising by anyone looking over my shoulder. If you work with word processing, you probably recognize your own threshold between minor editing and major revision when you assign your manuscript a new date, title, or code number.

Editing occurs in countless ways, and any serious researcher-cum-author should experience many of them. One way to gain editing experience that seems particularly well suited to academic and professional writing is through collegial review. I hope you recognize editing as help to be given to others as well as sought for yourself. Providing the service of editorial review for others not only gains you experience but also enlists you in our collective responsibility for the level of presentation in qualitative research. Editing the work of others also affords us an opportunity to recognize desirable and undesirable practices in their writing that we are not always able to discern in our own. If one's timing is right, graduate students polishing the final drafts of their dissertations are an especially receptive audience for editorial direction. The only cautions are to avoid the trap of editing for them rather than helping them become better author-editors on their own, and (as with the wheelbarrow instructions) to make sure that they have all the parts properly in place before they begin tightening.

Reading published book reviews provides another means for keeping tabs on colleagues' writing and offers a three-for-one return on your investment of time. First, you get an overview and critique of the content of new publications, which helps with the ever-pressing problem of keeping up in your field. Second, you get one academic author's reaction to the writing of another in the same field. Few reviewers can resist the temptation to comment on organization and style, although most insist or imply that they are above such things. Third, you sample the reviewer's own style, seen in a disciplined piece of writing addressing the delicate business of collegial (and sometimes not-so-collegial) review. Book reviews are an under-appreciated art form in academic writing. Read them. Write them.

When I edit my own material, I often experience a sense of diminishing return if I devote a too-sustained effort to the task. Manuscripts can always be improved (yes, this one too; how many more drafts to finally get it right?), and successive, productive editings are the means to accomplish it. But I also need distance from my words, lest I find myself changing text without necessarily improving it. When time permits, I put manuscripts on a figurative back burner for awhile, turning attention to other things before getting back to the editing. I do a better job of strengthening the interpretation, spotting discrepancies and repetitions, locating irregularities in sequence or logic, and discovering overworked words, phrases, and patterns after periods of benign neglect.

When time doesn't permit, I look for other ways to gain a fresh perspective. One is to edit backwards, last sections first. Others include reading aloud, reading a too-familiar manuscript in an unfamiliar setting, and reading a manuscript quickly—especially if all prior readings have been careful word-by-word ones. I was surprised to discover recently that simply changing the format of an article I had drafted (an easy trick with word processing) rearranged the spatial relationship of the words and gave a fresh perspective on sentences that were becoming fixed in my mind. Sometimes I go through a manuscript in mechanical fashion to see if I can eliminate one unnecessary word from every sentence, one unnecessary sentence from every page. When editing directly on the screen, if the bottom line of a paragraph contains only one or two words, I accept an implicit challenge to try to eliminate an equivalent number of characters somewhere within the paragraph to reduce the overall length of the manuscript by one line. I admit to wonderment and delight when I watch paragraphs literally tighten before my eyes!

Every sentence containing any form of the verb *to be* is a candidate for rewriting in active voice if I can see a way to do it. Often I cannot, which makes it all the more important to improve other sentences as I am able. As I become aware of them, I also go on "search and destroy" campaigns to ferret out overworked expressions and overused words. My current rampage is the word *very,* a very unnecessary word and habit. (In their popular *Elements of Style,* Strunk and White, 1972, p. 65, label *rather, very, little,* and *pretty* as "qualifiers" and offer this succinct advice: avoid them). A word habit I became conscious of during this writing is my overuse of *even.* I've always written with too many *buts,* but I have a hard time eliminating them. (Does that reflect a contrary nature?)

Having long ago discovered how (very) long it can take from the moment of first submission of a manuscript to finally seeing it in print, I continue revising drafts (even) after I submit them. (Remember: Only the final version counts!) I advise publishers of this edit-while-you-wait practice, offering to substitute a clean and current draft the moment a manuscript is to be put into production. Production is sometimes delayed for a year or two, and no draft can fail to be improved by periodic review during the waiting period. References may need to be updated. More important, you may be able to strengthen your interpretation or analysis during the time for reflection prompted by unanticipated delays. Recognize as well that your most profound insights may not occur for years. As the epigraph suggests, should you come to realize with the passage of time "how much the views on all points will have to be modified," you will still be in good company!

An invited article I once prepared for a prestigious audience of researchers suffered so many delays while the editor bullied and cajoled recalcitrant contributors that by the time the book was in print, a chapter intended as state-of-the-art looked more like a historical review. The lesson for me was to edit with an eye for a solid piece that will stand the test of time, rather than try to stay "up to the minute." Neither our qualitative studies nor our audiences have the sense of urgency about them one finds in some fields—all the more reason to make our contributions lasting ones, timeless rather than timely.

Seeking Formal Editorial Help

Among the sources of editorial help are the easily available but little-used talents of professional editors. In submitting material to a publisher, there is always the possibility that one will get such help free. Unfortunately, you cannot count on it. Nor can you predict either the nature or extent of in-house editorial help.

An author of my acquaintance submitted the draft of a book-length qualitative study to a university press eager to publish it. She was aghast to have her draft returned for approval in *final copyedited form* ready for the printer. What she had expected—counted on, really—was an editor's careful sentence-by-sentence examination to guide her own final editing. She had to make an agonizing decision (especially with a first book) to withdraw her manuscript, seek independent editorial help, and resubmit at a later date with the hope that the publisher's enthusiasm would not wane. Fortunately, it did not. The alternative to seemingly rigid deadlines (in this case, at least) was to counter with a superbly revised manuscript.

Matching editorial help offered with editorial help desired is uneasy business under any circumstances. As editor-in-chief of a scholarly journal for three years, my style was meticulous, and I encouraged our outside reviewers and in-house staff (a part-time professional editor and several graduate assistants) to be equally rigorous. We penciled comments and suggestions on every manuscript under serious consideration, usually circulating only one copy so that each of us was privy to suggestions made by earlier readers. (This was in part for our mutual edification. We read each other's comments and argued among ourselves – in the margins of the manuscript, if we thought it of interest to the author – whether our suggested changes were necessarily improvements.) Other than with format requirements, however, we never insisted on the changes we proposed, and we did not make a record copy of our suggestions. When manuscripts came back revised, as they almost always did, we read them anew rather than comparing them sentence by sentence with the earlier submission.

I was told that when we returned her manuscript, a colleague at another institution stormed out of her office and announced, "I haven't had anything marked up like this since I was a sophomore in high school." What we received at the editor's office, however, was a gracious thank-you for our careful reading and a much improved draft that we were pleased to publish. On another occasion, a contributor reacted upon seeing his article in print, "I didn't know I wrote that well!" Truth was, he didn't. But with our insistence and editorial suggestions, coupled with his willingness to rework the material, the results were fine. Because we insisted on better writing, we got it. I would be flattered someday to have an astute reader/critic discover and commend the caliber of writing in the journal during those years under my editorship, but that will never happen. Good writing does not call attention to itself, it enhances what is being written about.

That academic writers make such little use of free-lance editors can be attributed, I believe, to frugality coupled with lack of precedent. We seem willing to invest great amounts of time at our writing, but not a penny for editing. I do not recall ever seeing a line item budgeted for editorial assistance in a grant or project proposal, although the final product often is expected to be a publishable monograph or book rather than a technical report. There seems an unstated but prevailing notion that one's writing – like one's research – also should be original, entirely one's own. Too bad, when writing so benefits from review by others!

One can summon other arguments against hiring professional editorial help, in addition to the out-of-pocket-expense that academics would hardly dismiss as inconsequential. One problem is how to identify a good editor—the question of quality control in a field where virtually anyone who has ever written for publication or has taken a few writing courses can feign expertise. Researchers also worry that the only help editors provide is with style; that editors have no appreciation for technical fields, and thus do not really "understand." Unfortunately, that can be turned into a serious indictment. One of our claims in qualitative research is that we help others to understand themselves by seeing things through the perspective we provide. Editors ought to be able to help us accomplish our own stated purposes. Good editors should do it without bruising tender egos, at the same time fostering development of our individual styles. If your only reviewer/critics are your best friends and closest colleagues, you may need to be reminded of the slogan adopted in advertising for Listerine mouthwash: "There are things your best friends won't tell you." Halitosis pales by comparison to the lasting impression of poor writing.

How Do You Conclude a Qualitative Study?

You don't. Give serious thought to dropping the idea that your final chapter must lead to a conclusion or that the account must build toward a dramatic climax. In the dichotomous thinking said to be typical of Americans, research is sometimes portrayed as being either decision-oriented or conclusion-oriented. Clearly some research is decision-oriented, but I am not sure that "conclusion-oriented" is adequate to describe the rest of it. In reporting qualitative work, I avoid the term *conclusion.* I do not want to work toward a grand flourish that might tempt me beyond the boundaries of the material I have been presenting or detract from the power (and exceed the limitations) of an individual case.

Qualitative researchers seem particularly vulnerable to the tendency—and urge—to go beyond reporting *what is* and to use their studies as platforms for making pronouncements of *what ought to be.* A critical divide separates the realm of the observable from the realm of values about good and better. This is not simply the matter of a big leap: You cannot bridge the chasm between the descriptive and the prescriptive without imposing someone's judgment, whether originating from the people in the setting ("What we really need around here . . ."), from expert opinion ("If these people knew what was good for them . . ."), or from the researcher's own assessment ("I cannot help wondering whether . . ."). True, there is an evaluative dimension to all description, but the antidote is restraint. The urge to lend personal opinion and judgment seems to become strongest when we start searching for the capstone with which to conclude our studies. You can recognize it creeping into your work (or, if you prefer, into mine) with the appearance of words like "should," "must," "need," or "ought." There is nothing wrong with offering your personal opinions or professional judgments—but be sure to label them as such, and to search out and acknowledge their origins in your thinking.

Ruth Benedict once observed that "American popular audiences crave solutions" (1946, p. 192). As both producers and consumers of research, we need to recognize our collective penchant for closure of some sort, especially for endings that are satisfying. How often do we read about films produced with multiple endings while producers argue over the one likely to draw the biggest box office? Every article in our weekly news magazines, every report for live, on-the-spot TV coverage has its dramatic tag line. The endings for qualitative studies do not have to be all that dramatic; they need only to be adequate for the occasion. Nothing more may be required than a sentence or two tucked into the last paragraph of the chapter dealing with analysis or interpretation.

My advice is to work toward a conservative closing statement that reviews succinctly what has been attempted, what has been learned, and what new questions have been raised. Do not abandon your case study in an effort to achieve a grand finale. I remind students that it is not necessary to push a canoe into the sunset at the end of every paper. Recognize and resist the temptation of dramatic but irrelevant endings or conclusions that raise issues never addressed in the research. Beginnings and endings are important; they deserve extra attention from the author because they tend to get extra attention from the reader. Look for ways to make them better without letting them get bigger. Rather than striving for closure, see if you can leave both yourself and your readers pondering the essential issues you have addressed. In time you may understand more. Only in my 1989 Afterword to *A Kwakiutl Village and School* did I find an adequate way to conceptualize and in that sense conclude the study. Lapsed time: a quarter of a century!

Be prepared, however, that the point at which you would prefer to stop may not go far enough to satisfy your readers. Commercial publishers often boast that they "know their audience" and may insist that you offer more by way of a satisfying conclusion or set of summary points. If you argue that the case stands by itself, or that the lessons are not all that clear, then you may be pressed (by a wily publisher or editor, a granting agency, even a dissertation committee) to state what *you* learned, or to reflect on what *you* think it all means. Alternatives to a formal conclusion include summaries, recommendations or implications, or a statement of personal reflections. Any compatible combination of these alternatives may satisfy the need for closure without tempting you to go too far, losing your audience just as the final curtain descends. I remark briefly about each, because they raise critical questions about purposes and opportunities in qualitative research.

SUMMARIES

Concluding with a summary invites both the redundancy and the evaluative stance you may have been working to avoid. Yet a summary also may accommodate the very repetition and disclosure necessary to ensure that your message gets across in the form you intended. Descriptive case studies can be maddeningly ambiguous. Is that how you intend yours?

A summary can provide a careful, conservative way to conclude on a strong note. It allows a review of what you have done in terms of your original statement of purpose. It also provides an opportunity to anticipate critical reaction by pointing out shortcomings, discussing how you might have proceeded now that you are a bit older but wiser.

If the idea of a summary appeals to you, consider doing even more by providing brief summaries throughout the study rather than saving everything for the end. Most authors could make better use of chapter or section summaries if they really used them to summarize. Final sections labeled as summaries too often preview what is coming next rather than fulfill the promise of a succinct review of material already presented. Introductions, as the word suggests, belong at the beginning of new sections, not at the close of preceding ones. Concise and well-written chapter summaries provide a sort of running "box score" for stating how things stood at the beginning of the chapter and reviewing information and insights newly added. Summaries should help everyone remain on target, reader and author alike.

An "executive summary" or "guide to the reader" is a special kind of summary ordinarily found in the opening pages of a study rather than in the closing ones, often preempting more traditional front matter. An executive summary should outline the scope of the work and encapsulate the findings. If it is truly a *guide* for the reader (rather than an abstract in disguise), it also may indicate where to locate specific topics within the text.

An effective summary of this latter type appears in a monograph by Murray and Rosalie Wax and Robert Dumont, Jr., *Formal Education in an American Indian Community* (1964/1989). The entire study, consisting of only 126 pages—including 11 pages of appendix—stands as a model of field research and succinct reporting, particularly for its effort to reach an audience of practitioners via a scholarly monograph. Yet even with so brief a report, the authors immediately catch the reader's attention with a three paragraph (double-spaced, even on the printed page!) "Guide to the Reader" to convey the gist of their message to those who may not pause long enough to discern it for themselves. The opening paragraph of their guide appears in Figure 4.1. The special reading assignment for "skeptics and critics" that appears in the final sentence reflected a recognition by the senior authors (sociologist Murray Wax, anthropologist Rosalie Wax) that their qualitatively oriented approach was likely to be subject to scrutiny by methodologists but of little concern to busy practitioners.

RECOMMENDATIONS AND IMPLICATIONS

A frequent practice in resolving the how-to-conclude question is to prepare a final section or chapter that couples a brief summary with recommendations or implications. Whether boldly to offer recommendations or more tentatively to tease out implications depends on the nature and purpose of the study, its intended audiences, and the style or pose of the researcher (e.g., dispassionate observer, consultant, critic, advocate). In any case, we ordinarily see recommendations *or* implications, not the two together.

The press to offer recommendations can put the more scientifically oriented researcher in a bind: One would like to present the case so well, so thoroughly, and so fairly that the reader has the same basis for making judgments as the researcher—and, thus, the researcher is relieved of that responsibility. At the same time, when one has devoted extensive attention to a problem or setting (e.g., Why don't the children

Figure 4.1. Example of an Effective Executive Summary

A GUIDE TO THE READER

Those who must skim the pages of reports as they run from crisis to meeting to office are advised to turn to the chapter titled "Summary and Recommendations," which has been written with them in mind. Readers who wish to examine a picture of a contemporary Indian reservation and who are indifferent to the preliminaries of a research investigation are advised to turn to the second chapter, titled "Ecology, Economy, and Educational Achievement." Skeptics and critics will want to read not only the first chapter ["Perspective and Objectives of this Research"] but also the Appendix ["Research Procedure"] before proceeding into the heart of the text.

SOURCE: Wax, Wax, and Dumont (1964/1989, p. v; titles in brackets added).

of this _____ [ethnic minority of your choice] group perform better in school? What steps could be taken to curb the _____ [social problem of your choice] among these teenagers? What might be done to improve the _____ [socially desirable goal of your choice] among members of this group?), it is not unreasonable for those involved to expect some kind of helpful reflections or advice.

The bottom line for practitioners is always, "So what?" A qualitative researcher's efforts to convey nonjudgmental objectivity is likely to be perceived instead as a typical academic cop-out. We may prefer not to be pressed for our personal reactions and opinions, but we must be prepared to offer them. It is not unreasonable to expect researchers to have something to contribute as a result of their studied detachment and inquiry-oriented perspective.

One way to provide that sought-after help is to outline the kind of additional information or insight a researcher would require in order to pose a solution, offer a recommendation, or render the kind of judgment requested. Treated too cavalierly, or brushed aside with an unbecoming modesty ("Oh, we couldn't possibly say anything about that—we don't know enough yet"), the too-humble-to-be-helpful approach can indeed be a cop-out. On the other hand, pointing to elements the researcher feels he or she has not understood, or that seem poorly defined, may help uncover inherent ambiguities. To the question, "Why don't you tell us how to make this program more effective?" a researcher may reply with a discomforting but not altogether unlikely explanation: "Because I have been unable to get a clear sense of what it is you are trying to accomplish." (My own efforts to describe an ambiguously defined community development project are reported in Wolcott, 1983b).

A second way to offer help—although it, too, can lead to discomfort and denial—is to identify seeming paradoxes. The manner in which people go about things often produces different, and sometimes opposite, effects from what they intend. Anthropologist Ray McDermott provides an example in his microcultural description and analysis of differences in the organization of reading instruction for the top and bottom pupils in one first-grade classroom. He observed how the top readers practiced their reading skills while the bottom readers rehearsed classroom protocols appropriate to their niche as "poor" students (McDermott, 1976). Although such an observation and interpretation might bring little joy to a dedicated but harried first-grade teacher, comparable paradoxes permeate formal education whenever the quick get the lecture and the slow get lectured.

A third way to offer help is to identify alternatives to current practice (or solutions to current problems) and to assist those responsible for action, or those who may be affected by it, in examining the possible consequences of these alternatives. In this way, the analytical skills of the researcher may serve not only as a potential resource for readers but also as a potential model for them in conducting further inquiry on their own.

The logical extension of this argument is that change agents—nurses, police officers, social workers, teachers, and so forth—should be collaborative partners in qualitative research, and ultimately should become researchers who conduct their own studies among their clients. Our problems with data overload should help us understand why an idea that sounds so right is generally so impractical. To an even greater extent than do researchers, practitioners must "get rid of" (which in this case means ignore) massive amounts of information about their clients, their settings, cultural differences, and so on before they can get on with their appointed tasks. To know more may hopelessly complicate assignments already hopelessly complex.

Drawing implications is akin to stating recommendations but allows the researcher to remain more distant and contemplative. If one wishes to address specialist audiences (e.g., practitioners, administrators, policymakers, other researchers) – including audiences whose members might not take kindly to boldly stated advice based on a neophyte researcher's modest study of a single case – then tentatively identifying *possible* implications may offer an oblique approach in which questions are posed rather than answered.

When our intended audience consists solely of research colleagues, I think it sufficient to conclude with a statement summarizing what has been learned and what appear to be the next steps in an ongoing process of inquiry. We like to think that we do more than simply talk to ourselves, however, and we must be prepared to say more, to offer what help we can. Most certainly we can do a better job of inquiring systematically into the kind of help that practitioners, administrators, and perhaps even those policymakers we are forever enjoining to heed our work really want. One of the intriguing questions constantly before us – our own professional paradox – is why social research has so little impact. Are we scratching where it isn't itching? Stated more anthropologically (i.e., rephrased without the value judgment), have we given adequate attention to the impact of our research efforts and to the related question of whether that is the impact we want to have?

PERSONAL REFLECTIONS

I welcome the current mood that encourages researchers to be candid and "self-reflexive" about fieldwork and also recognizes that the fieldworker is likely to be the individual most affected by the experience. Nonetheless, if you close on a note of personal reflection, keep the subject(s) of your study the focus of your reflections. The more you feel an urge to step into the spotlight, the more you should consider divorcing your reflections from the research. Write them up separately, especially if your presence and feelings have been muted elsewhere in the account. On the other hand, if you have maintained a presence, you have had opportunities to share your personal reflections all along; you probably have said enough. (See the discussion of two contrasting styles of researcher-reflective reporting, the *confessional* and the *impressionist,* in Van Maanen, 1988, chapters 4 and 5.)

Running Out of Space

"When in doubt, leave it out," the guidebooks advise novice travelers packing for an extended trip. Good advice for qualitative researchers, too – except that doubt is one of our pervasive concerns. How much description is enough to earn the accolade "thick description"? How much context is enough to make a study "contextual"? To avoid being shallow, how deeply must we delve to present a case "in depth"? At the other extreme, if luminaries like Malinowski and Margaret Mead can be faulted for "haphazard descriptiveness" (noted in Marcus and Fischer, 1986, p. 56), how can we assure that our own descriptiveness is of some higher order?

Faced with the dilemma of having more to pack than a suitcase can possibly hold, the novice traveler has three possibilities: rearrange so as to get more in, remove nonessentials, or find a larger suitcase. Qualitative researchers have comparable options. Like learning to pack small items inside bigger ones, there are ways to pack more into a manuscript without increasing its length. "Tightening" suggests that the end product will be more compact, although my experience is that unless revision is undertaken specifically to reduce manuscript length, deletions usually are matched by seemingly minor changes and additions that leave total manuscript length about the same—or a tad longer. If clever repacking is not remedy enough, some items will have to be left out. As to the third possibility, seasoned travelers and researchers alike are aware that large containers are unwieldy, often require special handling that entails additional costs, and may be prohibited by regulation (recall my instructions for this monograph: a "strict limit of 100-120 double-spaced manuscript pages").

Under two headings that follow ("Crowding More In" and "Cutting More Out") I offer suggestions of a mechanical nature for meeting space limitations. The underlying concern is not mechanical, however; it is an issue of focus. This is why I keep returning to the importance of the problem statement ("The purpose of this study is . . .") and reiterating that the problem statement itself must remain under continual critical review.

Given lingering doubts about the criteria of inclusion for descriptive studies, I can offer another aphorism that has served to guide my writing and that I have repeated frequently to help others experiencing difficulties with organizing, writing, or editing: *Do less, more thoroughly.* For years I wrongly attributed this to Alfred North Whitehead, although he most certainly was my inspiration if I inadvertently coined a phrase of my own. Whitehead's actual statement was delivered as two educational commandments: "Do not teach too many subjects," and "What you teach, teach thoroughly" (Whitehead, 1929/1949, p. 14).

"Do less, more thoroughly" is my maxim, and the zoom lens on a camera provides an analogy for the principle in action. If you want to take in more of the picture, you must sacrifice closeness of detail, and vice versa. Michael Agar suggests what he calls the "funnel approach" to fieldwork: "The strategy is to *selectively* narrow the focus within a previously explored broad field" (Agar, 1980, p. 9; for another lens analogy, see Peacock, 1986).

And do you have the focus right? The answer to that crucial question lies not within the research setting, and not within your choice of method; it is something you must bring *to* the setting. In the process of "selectively narrowing the focus" you will come to appreciate the value of both a solid grounding in an academic tradition and an orientation within an arena of professional concern. Even holistic ethnographers are spared responsibility for getting "everything." They look at what other ethnographers look at, guided in a broad sense by the canons of cultural anthropology and in a specific sense by the problem they have set. Biographers, economic developers, health professionals, and sports pedagogues all have their own concerns. Nobody has to get it all. "A way of seeing is always a way of not seeing," Kenneth Burke (1935, p. 70) once observed. Selective focusing helps to accomplish both at once.

CROWDING MORE IN

Qualitative research weds us to prose. We need to remind ourselves that charts, diagrams, maps, tables, and photographs not only provide valuable supplements to printed text but can condense and expedite the presentation of supporting detail.

I have revealed my inclination to "think sections," "think chapters," or "think table of contents" from the moment I begin a new study. That advice can be restated more universally, applicable to the presentation of quantitative and qualitative data alike. As Miles and Huberman state it: "Think display" (1984, p. 21 passim; see also Tufte, 1983). Display formats provide alternatives for coping with two of our most critical tasks, data reduction and data analysis.

Charts and diagrams offer other ways to give our thoughts embodiment. They invite us to sort and categorize data, to explore what goes with what, and to contemplate how seemingly discrete data may be linked in previously unrecognized ways. Researchers who think spatially work through their charts and diagrams in order literally to "see" their studies before them, whereas most of us are constrained by the regimented vision of prose. Some qualitative researchers conceptualize and work systematically through their studies with huge charts and diagrams drawn on inexpensive newsprint spread across their walls or floors.

In more conventional formats, tables and charts also can relay information that provides context for a study but is of interest to only a small proportion of one's anticipated audience. Similarly, maps are an expedient way to locate a region and community, sketch maps are a convenient way to plot movement or show before-and-after comparisons, and pictures are still worth a thousand words (more or less, and assuming that they raise no insurmountable issues with confidentiality or permissions).

Graphics also enhance the likelihood of capturing the attention of readers who "see" facts or visualize relationships in other ways. They also keep us mindful of exploring alternative forms of representation and presentation by augmenting the always potentially tedious flow of words on the printed page. Display has a function in data analysis as well: Charts and diagrams developed in rough form as a preliminary way to organize (and get rid of) data can help researchers tease out relationships and patterns spatially. They facilitate the management and analysis, as well as the presentation, of data. Don't hesitate to explore alternative ways—and shapes—for displaying and summarizing data using tables, diagrams, figures, and maps.

By way of example, I include here (Figure 4.2) a working diagram that offers visual representation of a variety of approaches to on-site research. My original purpose for organizing this material was to identify a number of strategies so that students new to qualitative research would not invariably affix the label *ethnography* to their studies merely because they were unaware of the wide range of alternative terms and approaches. Initially I condensed some brief comparative material describing each approach into a columnar table (Wolcott, 1982). The table, however, lent an unfortunate rigidity to its contents. I wanted to convey a sense of the interrelatedness among the approaches without implying a hierarchy. A pie chart provides an alternative way to organize the information, suggest that interrelatedness, and aid my effort to identify and arrange the elements. Note that there are already more words in this paragraph than in the figure, which is another part of my message: the chart speaks for itself.

Figure 4.2. Qualitative/Descriptive Studies Organized by Research Approach

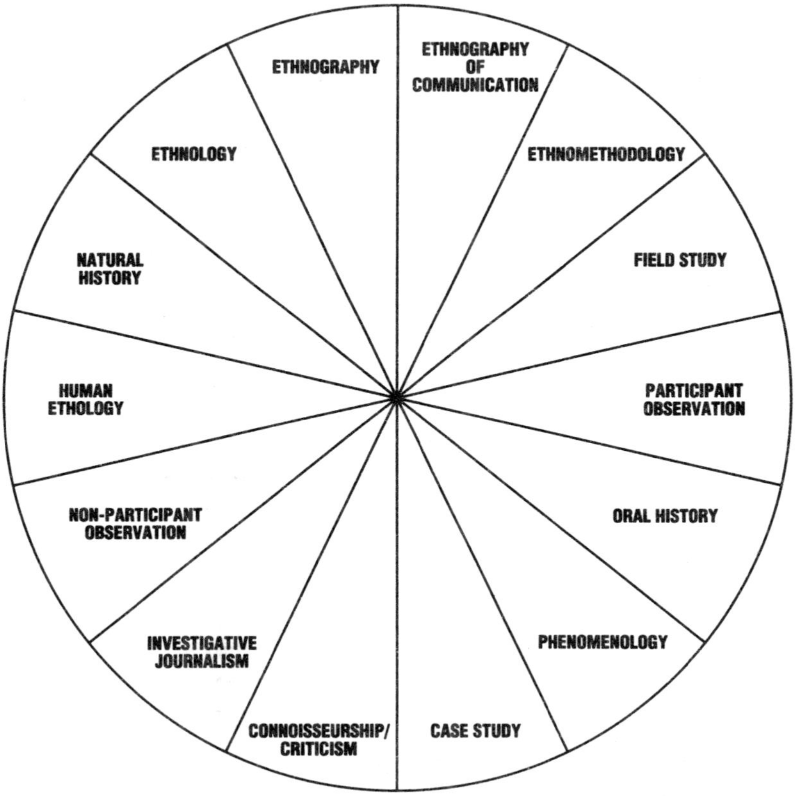

SOURCE: Wolcott (1982), with revisions.

That the chart speaks for itself happens to be both a fact and a condition for material that appears separate from the text: text and alternatives to it stand independently of each other. Supplementary material must be labeled adequately to be understood without having to consult the text. Obviously, this is accomplished with captions and subheadings. The problem is to ensure that the material is self-explanatory, not text dependent. To determine whether your charts and tables stand by themselves, see if someone unfamiliar with the text can interpret your visual displays correctly.

As with prose, tables, charts, and photographs also require continuous review. Nothing should be considered for inclusion that is not of high quality (i.e., clean lines, sharp focus), but materials also must be relevant and complementary to the purposes at hand, not there simply to break up space or create an impression. As revising and editing continue, so should review of supporting materials. They will be reviewed critically by a publisher as well, for they increase production costs and you may be asked to justify the added expense.

Charts or tables critical to early drafts sometimes become superfluous after the writing is completed. Conversely, maps and diagrams may have to be simplified to be effective. Several maps may be needed to accomplish competing purposes originally designed to be achieved in one (e.g., locating the region of study in one map, accompanied by a map of larger scale providing finer detail). In a word, everything should be orchestrated. Don't leave the reader wondering why something was included that seems to have no bearing on the purposes of the study.

A word of caution: charts and tables provide a ready trap for authors vulnerable to attacks of "misplaced concreteness" (another phrase prompted by Whitehead, although his concern was with abstraction rather than specificity, as implied here). The problem of misplaced concreteness is not limited to charts and tables, of course; it arises whenever detail is introduced at a distracting level inconsistent with the purposes of a study or with the level of detail provided elsewhere. Biographers and historians seem particularly susceptible to misplaced concreteness, faced (dare I say preoccupied?) as they are with conflicting evidence and sometimes seeming to include data for no apparent reason except that they were uncovered during the search process. The most flagrant example of misplaced concreteness that I recall, however, appeared in a sociological study in which the appendix to a modest monograph on social practices related to urban African beer drinking was a table of random numbers. The intended message, I assume, was "This is science." My reaction as reviewer was, "This is ridiculous."

Another practice among qualitative researchers for keeping manuscripts to a reasonable length is to provide only brief excerpts from interviews or field notes in the narrative but to include longer protocols in an appendix or supplement, a practice I discuss briefly in the next chapter. Shifting data from one place to another does not change the overall length of a manuscript; it relocates the problem rather than alleviating it. Editorially, however, this can be effective for lending emphasis and focus. There is a misguided tendency among qualitative researchers to let informants rattle on in the written account just as they may have done during their interviews. The consequence is often counterproductive, leaving readers bored rather than beguiled. At times informants do need to be given their voice, and there are approaches such as the anthropological life history in which that voice may be the only one heard. In general, however, I feel that brief quotes are more effective than lengthy ones, especially when multiple speakers are being quoted on the same issue. The longer your quoted passages (whether from informants or printed sources), the greater the need to be sure readers understand the point that *you* are making.

CUTTING MORE OUT

When outside readers agree that some section of a manuscript can be deleted, I hasten to follow their recommendation. Even with general consensus about the need for cutting, however, my experience is that readers will disagree about what should go and what should stay. If cutting is both major and mandatory, I appreciate the authoritative voice and experience of an editor for suggestions about how to proceed. I also have discovered that readers of early drafts are not reluctant to identify possible cuts if I first reassure them that my problem is no longer whether to cut, but where.

Whatever the motivation for cutting—the recommendations (or insistence) of others, or an intuitive feeling of your own—you will be better off to do the actual cutting and necessary rewriting yourself rather than to delegate it. If you do not have access to critical readers to help identify possible ways to cut, let me suggest some places that seem to yield most easily if you have trouble getting started.

First, look for little diatribes where you may have gone off on a tangent. These become easier to identify after you gain some distance from a manuscript. You may suddenly realize that certain questions or issues were dropped rather than developed, or that you took advantage of an opportunity to get on a soapbox about a topic of perennial concern. Concern to you, that is—but perhaps not to your readers. Colleagues can usually spot such detours if you specifically ask, but may be too polite to mention them if you do not; they are already familiar with you and your ways.

Second, make a critical assessment of all points supported with multiple illustrations, multiple vignettes, or multiple quotations, with a sharp eye for needless duplication. Save the best and drop the rest. Summarize the general pattern you see, retaining only an illustration or two. You may be attempting to preserve and portray important nuances you recognize in closely related examples, but subtle differences are likely to go unrecognized by readers who do not share your first-hand experience. Most of us see and hear our informants as we enter their words onto a manuscript. We forget that our readers cannot do that; for them, the words remain lifeless on the page, and the repetition of materials that are virtually identical becomes tedious.

Do not be bashful, however, about including an excess of illustrative material in your early drafts. It is easier to synthesize or delete from too many examples than to go back through notes searching for the perfect illustration dropped too soon. Further, your choice of quotes and vignettes may change as the text develops and you look for effective ways to communicate and illustrate points. Be sure to code your excerpts (preferably right in your manuscript where they appear) so that you can locate original sources efficiently. Your coding system also can be used to relay important information to your reader in encapsulated form (e.g., "Field notes 11/8/84" or "M-33-6th" [male, 33-years-old, 6th grade teacher]).

Third, carefully examine every "beginning": the first sentence and paragraph of each chapter or section, the first section of every chapter, and the entire first chapter itself. In rereading my own drafts, I have discovered that my start-ups are often warm-ups; they help me but do nothing for readers who instead may be cooled out by a slow start. You may be able to lop a bit off *every* beginning—unless, of course, you heeded my advice to plunge into your account with that key sentence, "The purpose of this study is . . ." (Several readers of early drafts asked why I hadn't begun this monograph that way, politely hinting that my Chapter 1, brief as it is, still seemed a slow start.)

Finally, look for whole intact sections—even entire chapters—that might be dropped or relegated to a separate writing project. To your surprise, you may discover that huge chunks can be deleted where smaller pieces cannot. Deleting big chunks may leave glaring gaps that you can point to as major topics intentionally passed over, to be dealt with at another time. (To stay within space limitations, at the suggestion of the editors I deleted two chapters from this monograph, each of which subsequently was developed into a separate article. I'll bet you never missed them.) By contrast, fiddling with minor cuts may leave you feeling anxious that the account is becoming choppy and disjointed, perhaps even losing its integrity. Pruning stimulates growth, our gardening friends tell us. Editorial "pruning" ought also to be invigorating, to author and manuscript alike. Keep an intact copy of the original version; unlike the gardener, should your initial efforts seem a bit severe you can easily undo them or try different possibilities.

How to fit qualitative/descriptive research into the prescribed limits of journal-length articles or monograph-length series, or how to compress two years of fieldwork and writing into a 15-minute time slot in a symposium, is vexing indeed. David Fetterman reports a case where program management objected to the brevity of an evaluation report he had drafted, but he notes that the objection was based on the belief that "a physically weightier document would be more useful to them to sell the program in the future" (1989, p. 17). This may be the only recorded case where someone wanted a qualitative researcher to write more, rather than less.

Faced repeatedly with this dilemma of having to compress qualitative reporting, both in my own writing and in trying to help others, my resolution, advice, and philosophy is summed up in the idea of "doing less more thoroughly." A strategy for accomplishing this is to look for parts, instances, or cases that can stand for the whole. Reporting parts is all you can possibly do in a journal article or brief symposium paper, but it is a reasonable guideline for developing a full-blown study as well.

Do you remember Alfred's dilemma described at the end of Chapter 2? (I'll bet you do. We tend to remember material presented through anecdotes and personal asides.) If Alfred comes seeking my advice, I'll ask if he has considered taking some manageable "unit of one" for a focus, some portion of the year's activities that would allow him to represent what he has fathomed from his extended data collecting without having to recapitulate that entire year. Might he construct his study around *one* student in the class rather than all of them; meticulously analyze *one* day in class rather than every day; dissect *one* social studies unit from inception to posttest rather than try to review all the units presented during the year; analyze *one* critical event rather than regard everything that occurred as critical?

Returning to the zoom-lens analogy, one way to keep a descriptive study manageable is to zoom in progressively closer and closer until your descriptive task is manageable, then zoom back out again to regain perspective. Like a viewer, a reader, too, needs context to know where the single case fits into the larger scheme of things. So what can we learn from studying only one example or one aspect of anything? My answer may seem facile, but I stake my career on it as a qualitative researcher: All we can!

5. FINISHING UP

The materials that precede and follow the main body of text in a monograph or book are known by rather unimaginative labels: front matter (also "preliminaries") and back matter (or "end matter"). In abbreviated fashion, many of these "matters" must be attended to in journal articles, reports, and chapters in edited collections as well. I introduce and discuss them below in checklist fashion in the order they usually appear in a publication, although that differs from the order in which they ordinarily are addressed.

It is both a courtesy and good politics to be familiar with the format of a journal or monograph series and to submit material in the manner requested. Editors can rightly insist that you do. As noted, you will discover a wide range of practices and preferences from one publisher, one professional field, and one journal to the next, and practices often vary dramatically from one editor's tenure to the next with the same journal, even when policy statements remain the same. It is the business of an editorial staff to establish the kind and extent of uniformity desired. For the author, this may leave little or no choice. You may face some unexpected writing to complete and some unanticipated decisions to make; you also will find that many important decisions have already been made for you.

TITLE

A shorthand title may serve adequately and efficiently in the early stages of a project. That working title, and the date of your current draft, should appear on every page. If your working title encapsulates your problem statement and serves as a constant reminder about focus, so much the better. From the outset, be thinking about an effective final title and jot ideas for possible titles in your notes. During the long interim between the start-up of a project and a completed first draft, the title is one of the few tangible aspects you can share that both announces and summarizes your study. In his reflective article "From Title to Title," Alan Peshkin—whose several book-length studies on aspects of

American communities and education provide excellent models of qualitative research—describes how the evolving sequence of tentative titles during the course of a field study reveals his thought processes as he progressively redefines and focuses his research (Peshkin, 1985).

Selecting a title is both serious work and fun. A perhaps unfortunate but nonetheless common practice in scholarly writing is to assign what amounts to a double title. As a consequence, two long, independent, and sometimes seemingly unrelated titles, joined by a colon, get attached to even the shortest of articles. Often one of these titles is creative, even catchy, although I caution against being too cute; titles can come back to haunt you and may detract from your intent. If your first title is a bit on the clever side, its complement, the subtitle (or label, if you think of it that way), should accurately convey the nature of your work.

My friend Norman Delue and I are credited by Ron Rohner for suggesting *They Love Me, They Love Me Not* (Rohner, 1975) as the title for his then-newly-completed manuscript, but our creative inspiration would have done a grave disservice without his complementary subtitle, *A Worldwide Study of the Effects of Parental Acceptance and Rejection.* Similarly, *Teachers Versus Technocrats* (Wolcott, 1977) has proven an effective title for one of my studies, but it sorely needed its subtitle, *An Educational Innovation in Anthropological Perspective,* to bring it to the attention of the right audience, although the subtitle is a mouthful.

Should a Hollywood studio approach me about making a film based on this monograph, I'll cast about for a snappier title ("Romancing the Keys?"). Until they do, however, my conscience is clear—the title succinctly and accurately conveys enough of the content to hold its own in the marketplace of ideas. It is short but not too short to communicate. Short titles sometimes render a disservice. One that comes to mind is Gregory Bateson's succinct *Naven* (Bateson, 1936). Although recognized today as an "eccentric classic" (Geertz, 1988, p. 17), the book's title only compounded the obscurity in which it remained shrouded for more than two decades.

DEDICATION

My personal view is that we've gone overboard with the well-intended but subject-to-abuse ritual of dedicating works, particularly works of limited scope and modest appeal. My recommendation is to *acknowledge* the help and support of others (including those spouses and offspring who, it would seem, somehow manage to convey their suffering after all) rather than overdo it with dedications. I think dedications should be reserved for the finest of our works and the most special of people. With lots of special people in mind, I have been able to resist encumbering anyone with a dedication thus far, and I intend to hold out a bit longer.

PREFACE

Prefaces are fine as an idea, but their placement in a document seems unfortunate. Although written last, often in a style too revealing and personal for an author we have not met, they are located where they will be read first. As author, you may want the opportunity to talk in a direct, personal way to your readers, but I suggest you do it later. If you have reflections to share as a result of your writing, save them for last, when readers will know what you are talking about and may appreciate an opportunity to know you better. In lieu of a preface, consider closing with personal reflections or a final note to serve as the postscript, or incorporate the more methodologically relevant of your reflections into your closing statement, as discussed previously.

INTRODUCTION AND FOREWORD

Preparing an introduction or foreword presents authors with yet another temptation for academic throat-clearing. I recommend against including either, unless someone else has been invited to prepare it. Chapter one, page one, is where the author should first address the reader, and nothing should stand in the way of their meeting on that page immediately. What is written later by way of reflection should appear later, rather than distract or detract. If more explaining is necessary, then the introduction itself probably needs to be rewritten.

ACKNOWLEDGMENTS

I received an early lesson about acknowledging others from my mentor George Spindler. The Spindlers were houseguests visiting me after I took a full-time academic appointment upon completion of doctoral studies. I eagerly shared an early draft of a chapter I had been invited to write, tentatively titled "Concomitant Learning." Spindler was up early the next morning, but to my disappointment I found him looking through materials he had written (my library contained many of them) rather than reading my new draft. He had already read and enjoyed my article, he explained, but he expressed disappointment at my failure to credit him as source or inspiration for the concept that provided my title and rationale. He had been searching for the citation I should have made. "But you've never written about it," I explained, reaffirming what I already knew and he was beginning to suspect. "I got the idea from you, but you only suggested it in a seminar. There was no publication to cite."

Technically (and luckily) I was correct, as his search revealed. That wasn't the entire lesson, however. "No matter where or how you encounter them," he counseled, "always give credit for the sources of your ideas. It's so easy to do; so appropriate to good scholarship . . . and so appreciated." Never again have I limited my acknowledgments only to people whose ideas are in print. And I, too, have "so appreciated" that courtesy when extended to me!

As with much of the front matter, however, acknowledgments also can be placed at the end rather than at the beginning of the text, and that is where I recommend putting them. They are less distracting there, and by then readers will better understand what is being acknowledged. In many scholarly journals a preferred form for general acknowledgments (e.g., inspiration, reviewers of early drafts) is to contain them in a first and unnumbered endnote, followed by numbered endnotes that, among other things, may include additional acknowledgments or permissions.

I make an effort to share as much credit as I can without compromising any confidentiality necessary for the research itself. An idea borrowed from novelist James Michener is to keep lists of those who help at each stage of the work and to acknowledge their contribution in the same sequence. I keep a log of the names of people who assist in any important way during the entire course of a study or preparation of a manuscript, not just those involved with the final draft. It took seven paragraphs to acknowledge the help I received with the research and revisions of *Teachers Versus Technocrats,* yet I do not recall anyone faulting *that* section as overwritten.

TABLE OF CONTENTS

I have already extolled the virtues of preparing a working draft of a table of contents as a valuable tool, not only for organizing data but for organizing the field research as well. In the final stages of preparing a book-length study, the original table of contents, with its chapter headings and subheadings, needs review in terms of appropriate titles, parallel treatment of like categories, and an orderly sequence for unfolding the account. The best way to give a critical appraisal is to make a separate list of all headings and subheadings and examine them in relation to each other. Do they provide an adequate structure to hold the account together? Authors of briefer statements (articles, chapters in an edited volume, research notes or brief communications in journals) should recognize that their headings and subheadings constitute an implicit table of contents deserving the same critical attention.

Preparing a formal table of contents presents another occasion for difficult decisions about level of detail. There are no fixed answers, but trade-offs between as much as possible and as little as possible are fairly easy to assess. If you do not provide an executive summary or some comparable guide for busy readers (i.e., those you suspect will read hurriedly, if at all), the table of contents provides the only indication of what you are presenting other than the title, except in rare cases when a back cover or book jacket provides summary information.

As a general guideline, the more concise the table of contents the better—preferably contained on a single page that serves at once as an outline and reader's guide. A problem with a brief, eye-catching, barebones table of contents, however, is that chapter headings by themselves are not likely to convey an adequate sense of the scope and depth of your research, particularly if you employ conventional chapter titles like Introduction, Method, Descriptive Account, Analysis, and Summary. Furthermore, if you do not include an index (dissertations never do, and neither do most qualitative/descriptive studies), the table of contents provides the only guide for anyone trying to locate material within the study. So there is a case for providing a detailed one.

How to decide between the alternatives? The issue is the same level-of-detail question that pervades all descriptive research: How much to include? Here, I think, is a case where more may be better, sacrificing elegance for completeness in order to draw attention to your work. In dissertations and unpublished reports, detailed tables of contents are not only appropriate but essential. As a compromise between too much and too little, you might consider making your chapter titles as helpfully descriptive as possible and then expanding individual chapter descriptions to the limit of what will fit comfortably on a single *printed* page. Among several books near at hand as I write, it appears that monographs and shorter, single-authored books tend to follow the one-page format, perhaps underscoring their succinctness; textbooks and edited collections sometimes have tables of contents that continue for several pages, staking an implicit claim to comprehensiveness.

FOOTNOTES AND ENDNOTES

Notes that accompany text properly are considered as text rather than as front or back matter. Nevertheless, with some publishers, certain traditions (e.g., biography, history), and most journals, they follow the text, usually appearing at the end of each separately authored article or chapter or at the back of an authored book. I doubt that current practice will change, but I seize every opportunity to voice my objection to (i.e., deliver a little diatribe about) separating notes from text. A major step in this direction is to embed in parentheses all references—to one's field notes or interviews; to sources formally cited; and to ideas gleaned from others—within the text where they appear. This can eliminate much of the need for footnotes. Do whatever possible to keep your other footnotes to a minimum, and to keep those you need as close as possible to the text.

Alas, you probably will not have any choice in these matters. They are questions of format and style dictated by tradition and, in journal publication, by economies of time and cost. It used to cost more to keep footnotes on the page corresponding with text because lines of type had to be moved (literally, by hand) to accommodate them. Computerization has virtually eliminated this as a technical problem, but old habits die hard and journals are as hidebound as academic disciplines in leaving things as they were. Journal articles are not usually so lengthy that it is a burden to locate accompanying notes printed at the end of an article. With longer works, however, I find it cumbersome to locate endnotes that follow each separate chapter and utterly exasperating to have to search for them if they have been picked up along the way and deposited at the back of a book.

Only for fields like history and biography that depend heavily on citations to other sources can I think of a convincing rationale for separating notes from text. Even there, the consequence—and resulting paradox—is that scholars writing in these traditions are forever interrupting themselves, sometimes giving their footnotes such attention that they take on a life of their own to comprise a study within a study. Although well established in the disciplines where it is practiced, excessive footnoting does not provide a good model for field-oriented researchers whose primary sources deserve primary billing.

I write early drafts without footnotes. I allow myself some excess in using parenthetical comments within sentences, occasionally writing a parenthetical paragraph as well. During revision, I reexamine these parenthetical comments to see if I can incorporate them into the text. Any remaining tangents, explanations, and asides then are reviewed with an eye for turning them into footnotes. My preference is to avoid footnotes entirely, but when circumstances (or editors) call for them, I review and edit them carefully. Some authors use footnotes effectively, and a few delight us with them, but I regard them as something of a habit-forming affectation in academic writing. Like underlining, using quotation marks to set off "cute" words, and the **boldface** now so readily available through word processing, footnoting can lose its effectiveness through overuse.

REFERENCES AND BIBLIOGRAPHY

The most important "back matter" in scholarly publishing is the section for references. For readers familiar with the literature in a particular field, an author's references provide a quick and fairly reliable guide to his or her disciplinary or professional orientation, as well as to the depth and currency of that orientation. When I need a quick gauge on unfamiliar authors, I look at their "quoting circle," the authors and works they in turn cite.

Although the two labels *references* and *bibliography* continue to be used somewhat interchangeably, a distinction between them is recognized widely. Bibliographies retain their traditional definition as lists of works on a subject, the kind of comprehensive but focused reader's guide prepared by librarians or anyone pursuing a specialized interest. There was a time in the not-too-distant past when a scholar making a new contribution in a field was expected to provide a comprehensive list of all previously published material as well. Those lists were properly called bibliographies. Today such Renaissance thoroughness is seldom seen and not ordinarily expected; it is increasingly difficult to remain up-to-date and in command of everything written, even in highly specialized subfields (and, as I suggested earlier, those who doggedly try to keep up with what everyone else is writing seldom find time for commensurate writing of their own).

As a result of the information explosion (in quantity, if not always in quality), bibliographic thoroughness associated with an earlier day has been replaced by expediency. Instead of compiling a comprehensive bibliography, we now ordinarily are expected to provide only a list of citations in a section titled "References" or "References Cited," the latter leaving little doubt about the criterion for inclusion.

Inexperienced authors often are caught unaware, and create extra work for conscientious editors (and some possible embarrassment for themselves) when informed that they have included among their references works not cited or—the complementary sin—have included citations in text for which no reference is provided. Inventorying such irregularities is one of the early and easiest tasks for a copy editor.

One drawback of current practice is that for any and every reference an author wants to include, a citation must appear somewhere in the text. Journal articles often contain a telltale sentence listing in perfunctory fashion all the ought-to-be-mentioned classics that, quite likely, will *not* be mentioned again. One alternative to this citation ritual is to combine the reference and bibliographic functions under a more flexible title such as "References and Select Bibliography" or "References and Further Reading." Another alternative, and the only option for complying with most journal formats, is to review the classics in a footnote specifically dedicated to identifying important prior works, perhaps situating one's intended contribution among them. Because citations made in footnotes also are included among the references, the classics receive due recognition without the shoddy treatment sometimes apparent when they are recited pro forma in the text.

Embedding citations in the text rather than in footnotes or endnotes not only reduces the need for footnoting but also weans us from the practice of employing Latin abbreviations unfamiliar to postmodern scholars. Today, in place of *ibid., loc. cit.,* or *op. cit.,* when a citation is to the same work as the immediately preceding one, only a page reference is required; when the citation is to a different author—including one cited earlier but not immediately preceding, or where there is any chance of confusion, or if the reader would have to search back in the text to find the source—simply repeat the author's name and year of publication, along with specific reference to page numbers, as appropriate.

If we now could get authors to stop putting a period after *et* when they abbreviate the phrase *et alia* in reference to multiple authors, our ignorance of Latin would no longer be so apparent. By the way, in the first citation to multiple-author works, *all* authors ordinarily ought to be identified, even if it seems that every graduate student on the project—or doctor in the hospital—got in on the act. In subsequent reference to the same citation, *et al.* is acceptable after listing the first author. Some guidelines suggest that you needn't list all authors (except for the full citation that must appear in the references) if there are more than six, but that seems arbitrary. On the other hand, multiple authorship itself is a strange practice, essentially a legacy from laboratory science in which authorship is associated with the theoretical or experimental work rather than the write-up. In qualitative research, where the writing can make or break a study, I prefer to see the principal author(s) identified as such. Collaborators, field assistants, or seminar members can be identified in the acknowledgments, where they do not confound citations or imply authorship.

As with many details discussed in this chapter, you probably will have no choice about reference style if your study is accepted for publication. An editor may send you a style sheet, refer you to a recent publication or journal issue, or point you to whichever style manual (and edition) currently serves as standard. Graduate schools typically expect dissertation writers to follow current practice in their field as exemplified in its leading journals.

Although you may have no discretion in selecting a style for a particular publication, these are discretionary matters, and you should recognize not only the variations but the traditions associated with them. I prefer the reference style of the *American Anthropologist,* not only because of its obvious link with the ethnographic tradition but for several mechanical reasons as well. It is clean (no quotation marks, parentheses, or underlines/italics unless they appear in the original), it is complete (no abbreviations; capitalization follows the original source; authors' full names may be used), and it is elegant (authors' names appear only once, on a separate line that precedes references to their individual works, listed chronologically).

Working in an anthropological tradition in the psychologically dominated field of educational research, I find it ironic whenever I am directed to redo my references in APA style (i.e., consistent with the *Publication Manual of the American Psychological Association,* now in its third edition, 1983), especially when presenting or discussing qualitative research. I recognize that APA provides a valuable service for authors and editors alike, just as the Modern Language Association of America does for authors in the humanities with its *MLA Handbook for Writers of Research Papers* (also in a third edition, 1988). Nevertheless, I recommend that researchers pursuing anthropologically oriented fieldwork know *AA* style and employ it if given a choice, just as

I expect people working in a sociologically oriented tradition to follow the style of one of the major journals in sociology.

APPENDIXES AND SUPPLEMENTS

Appendixes (or appendices, following the Latin) are auxiliary materials added at the back. Tables, charts, maps, and diagrams critical to the text ordinarily appear with it, but there may be additional material an author wishes to make available. A frequent practice among qualitative researchers is to excerpt relatively brief portions of important material—interviews, especially—in the text, and to include complete typescripts in an appendix. In that way, detailed information can be made available for the technical reader without burdening the account with lengthy transcripts. Similarly, interview schedules or questionnaires often are included in an appendix and, as noted, the discussion of method may be placed there, freeing the main body of text for description and interpretation.

Another use of the appendix is to provide illustrative case material or brief case histories that supplement the main text without interrupting the account. In situations where the expectations of one's audience are quantitatively oriented, but the researcher feels that descriptive data may provide important information and perspective as well, an appendix can supply the information without requiring explanation or apology. My hope would be that closet qualitative researchers, aware of the potential contribution these approaches have to make but reluctant to go public on their behalf, might see a progression in their own work: case histories or comparable descriptive material slipped unobtrusively into an appendix in one's earliest studies, subsequently given more prominence (e.g., incorporated into the main text), still later achieving chapter status, and eventually taking center stage. The progression from a rigidly quantitative approach to a primarily qualitative one in the careers of some research luminaries should not go unremarked.

The terms *supplement* or *supplementary materials* can be used interchangeably with *appendices.* If the additional materials are so voluminous that they are bound separately, they are usually labeled as a supplement. A caution: the bulkier those appendices or supplementary materials grow, the more you may need to ask yourself whether you still believe that data "speak for themselves." If data do speak for themselves, there ought to be a great demand for original field notes and full-length interview protocols. Is there?

INDEX AND KEY WORDS

I have never had to prepare an index. I understand it is an exhausting task (or was, prior to computerization) as well as something of a dying art. With the capabilities of word-processing programs, indexing may become a common practice once again. Although it appears to be reemerging in somewhat mindless, mechanical form, we are better off with indexes than without them.

You may be spared from having to index your own material, but do not remove yourself entirely from the process if someone is assigned to do it for you. You may want to delete or add categories apparent to you but not so obvious to a programmer or an indexer unfamiliar with your field. Similarly, if requested to supply key words or descriptors intended to assist in the task of indexing, select words or phrases designed to bring your work to the attention of others with shared professional interests. As a journal editor, I was surprised at how little thought authors appeared to give to our standing request for index words. We included key words with each article and used them in preparing an index for the volume year. Too few authors seemed able to put themselves in the position of a reader searching an index to locate relevant materials. For the *Anthropology and Education Quarterly,* as an example, *anthropology and education* was not particularly helpful as an index topic. Choose words and phrases that communicate your research problem or setting, rather than your fieldwork techniques. Think how little information is conveyed by *participant observation* as a locater term.

ABOUT THE AUTHOR

To whom do you think the task falls to prepare those brief but glowing sketches that accompany articles and chapters or appear on back covers and dust jackets? If you are asked to prepare a "bio," accept the assignment as another opportunity to enlist readers and to establish your authority to do the kind of research addressed in your report. What you say of yourself should link the study you have completed to your experience, your expertise, and your career; this is not the place to report your enjoyment of hiking or listening to music. Of your experience and past accomplishments, be specific and to the point. I appreciate authors who cite their *relevant* previous works by year and title, rather than those who claim to have published "several books and numerous articles on a wide variety of topics."

ABSTRACT

Having to encapsulate one's major professional preoccupation of the past months – or years – into the inviolable word limit of an article abstract for a journal, or of one's dissertation study for *Dissertation Abstracts,* can seem like the last straw. Fortunately, it *is* about the last straw, a signal to celebrate that a major project nears completion. As with anything you write about yourself as author, give time and thought to preparing your abstract, review it editorially, and try it out on others or ask them to read it aloud to you. An abstract can offer a valuable opportunity to inform a wide audience, to capture potential readers, and to expand your own interactive professional network. Whether others will pursue their reading may depend largely on their assessment of your abstract, including its style. Once again, emphasize your problem and content, not your fieldwork techniques.

PRINTER'S PROOFS

The rush I feel when I receive early proofs of a forthcoming work is at once literal, figurative, and ambivalent. After what always seems an inordinate delay, an author cannot help but wonder at receiving copyedited manuscript or printer's proofs by express mail with instructions to check and return everything within 72 hours! With printer's proofs, the rush is also sensory, often more exciting than seeing the finished product weeks or months later. At last, here it is in print. The ambivalence stems from the realization that the words are now set. In this final pass, your only responsibility is to ensure that what will appear in print corresponds with your manuscript. You can catch the printer's follies, but you must live with your own. If you are able to negotiate even minor changes, you may be required to accompany them with personal funds to cover additional costs that will be incurred. Most likely you will be instructed to make no changes. The lesson is straightforward and so is the moral: The time for editing is past.

Therefore, no matter how tired you may grow of your manuscript, or how anxious to be done with it, force yourself to make one last read-through of the final draft before you send it away. Visualize your words as though in print, for this *is* the version that counts. It is not too late to make changes, however, even if you must pen them neatly by hand. Then make your backup copies as you always do – one for the office, another for home – and mail it off. Whew!

6. GETTING PUBLISHED

Just about everyone in academia has opinions about, and a modicum of experience with, getting published. One way to locate a journal or publisher is to ask around among active and published researcher-colleagues to whom you have access. Another is to do some reading on this specific topic, such as Powell's (1985) informative case-study approach to understanding scholarly publishing, *Getting Into Print.* But prepare yourself: regardless of the magnitude of your just-completed research, and regardless of whether it was conducted pre- or post-Ph. D., it is not too likely that you will be successful in getting a book or monograph-length qualitative study published. You may have to settle for something less.

That is not to say you shouldn't try. There is always the chance of connecting with the right publisher or editor at the right moment. What I am suggesting is that in addition to looking for an outlet for a full-length study, you should also think about writing up smaller sections as journal articles. The fact that a full account exists—if only in your dissertation or a few xeroxed copies of your rewrite—frees you from having to recount everything while trying to say something. My advice is to draft the "full" version of a study first, then to consider how different, shorter pieces might be developed from it.

If your writing has been done with one eye on the promotion and tenure process, be aware that journal publication is ordinarily much faster than publishing a book or monograph. In my experience, new articles invited as chapters in edited volumes move even more slowly. Recognize also that long delays in publishing are not a good omen. New materials arrive all the time, new editors replace old ones. Manuscripts become less publishable the longer they sit, even when sitting in publishers' offices. Editorial promises get reinterpreted, forgotten, and sometimes flat-out broken.

But you must judge for yourself: I once had an enthusiastic academic editor tell me he was "interested" in publishing a book-length manuscript of mine in an existing monograph series. He lamented that at the time he did not have sufficient funds, and with an estimated 250 printed pages, plus photographs, he felt that the manuscript would be relatively expensive to publish. I wrote him off, interpreting his lament as a gracious rejection, but a rejection nonetheless. I began exploring other possibilities. I responded eagerly to another editor's reaction that, if slightly reconceptualized and greatly shortened, the manuscript might fit into his new series.

Unfortunately, the abridged and (too slightly, it seems) refocused study did not meet the second editor's expectations. I now had *two* monograph-length versions of my study, no publisher in sight, and a somewhat topical account rapidly becoming dated. In spite of its general social interest, I felt I should not invest more time on the study because its focus, the result of fieldwork in southern Africa during a year of sabbatical leave, was tangential to my scholarly interests except for the ethnographic experience itself. Then, unexpectedly, a letter arrived from the first editor informing me that he had been allocated additional funds and was preparing to put my manuscript into production. He wanted to know whether I had any last minute changes. From the outset he had every intention of publishing it! That's exactly what his letter said, when I reread it once more.

Academic publishing houses, like academic journals, tend to carve out their own special niche, preferring depth to breadth. The publisher most likely to publish your qualitative study is already publishing qualitative studies. Publishers who already publish studies most like yours are most likely to be interested in yours as well, unless what they already have in print is too similar to what you have written (rather than closely parallel, and thus complementary), or recent marketing experience has made them skittish. There is no reason not to try to dissuade them on either account. (Neither is there any reason to think you will be successful in doing so.) Review their publication lists and describe how your work will complement their existing titles rather than dilute their market. Authors are not particularly attentive to publishers; publishers are attentive to those who are.

While attending professional meetings, invest time at the book exhibits and search out publishers interested in the same topics and approaches that you are. Listen attentively to the dialogue at book exhibitor's stalls. Granted, most visitors are screening new materials for their teaching, looking for studies that augment their own research, or simply trying to keep up in their fields, if only by title and author. But broaden your gaze to include everyone at the scene, not just the consumers of research and the bright-eyed, bushy-tailed publishers' representatives there to ring up sales. Lurking somewhere nearby (perhaps not at the booth; maybe off talking privately with other authors, but available to meet with you by appointment) are the senior editors whose responsibility is literally to *buy* books (i.e., discuss manuscripts and ideas for them) rather than sell them. Their conversation is of a completely different sort: they visit congenially with their "authors in print," talk to authors with manuscripts (or ideas for them) about getting into print, and occasionally propose topics to prospective authors along lines the publisher feels might be productive. If there is any selling to be done, they expect authors to do it. Listen to those conversations and you will also realize how astute most commercial editors are, how knowledgeable they have become about what is being done in your field, and how helpful they can be—even if at times they dampen your enthusiasm or direct you to a competitor with a great idea you were certain they would covet for themselves.

Commercial publishers are oriented toward the adoption market. It can be disappointing to realize that a fine piece of research, beautifully written up, cannot be considered for publication because it will not "sell" (i.e., is not expected to command enough of the market to make publication feasible). What sells cannot be the only basis for conducting research, however—and clearly it is not. The market for qualitative studies is thin, oversaturated by our own successful efforts to convince publishers of potential markets that never quite materialize. My guess is that within each subfield a few studies—our own modest shelf of classics—account for most sales and are the studies to which we all point as precedents. Further, as Sage's editor Mitch Allen has observed (personal communication, March, 1989), "The writers of qualitative research are also the buyers of qualitative research. It is a closed system."

We would appear to be advantaged by having university presses as another publishing option, because ostensibly their mission is to advance scholarship rather than realize profits. In reality, I think the day has passed when university presses take chances on publishing materials with uncertain or thin markets. Increasingly, those presses not only have become self-supporting but are expected to make a return on the university's investment in them. Rather than serving as a fallback to guarantee that our studies will be published somewhere, university presses today seek the better stuff, which they further enhance with their imprimatur. Although in an earlier day university presses were instrumental in making publication possible in esoteric fields (most certainly including ethnography) today only about half a dozen devote attention to qualitative/descriptive work; they are the presses to know.

If you are seeking a publisher for your study, you are probably better off today to locate an appropriate *series* with a major publisher rather than to try to publish your work as a separate piece. An alternative is to find a small publishing house able to minimize risks by minimizing costs. In your eagerness to get published, don't lose sight of the fact that small publishing houses also have small budgets for advertising: one can publish *and* perish, in the sense of getting material into print that remains unknown. This is also the catch to the technological ease of desktop publishing: being able to publish your own study does not resolve the question of distribution, even when recovering out-of-pocket costs is not a major concern.

If you are successful in finding an interested publisher, your next reaction may be that the publication of your work seems to be one of the world's best-kept secrets. Rather than bemoaning the poor job your publisher is doing to promote your study, take responsibility to help spread the word. Send letters or announcements to your professional colleagues. Advise the publisher of journals to which your book should be sent for review (supply addresses and the names of the current book review editors, not just the names of the journals), and follow up independently to make sure that the material was received. You can probably badger your publisher into sending out more complimentary copies than is customary if you supply names, addresses, and a rationale.

The real key to the sales problem lies outside the scope of qualitative studies themselves: they are not adopted for classroom use on the scale that makes textbook publishing lucrative because they are not easy for instructors to use. They are neither self-teaching nor self-evident. They may make teaching more exciting, but they definitely make it more challenging. The only way to expand the market for qualitative/descriptive studies is by demonstrating their effective use in our own teaching. But that, as they say, is another story, maybe even another monograph: *Teaching (Teaching Up?) Qualitative Studies.* Our responsibility as authors/researchers is to make sure that, when needed, the studies are there, well researched and well written.

Alternative Ways To Get in Print

Although I confessed that I "think writing" from the outset of a study, and that I begin thinking about a proposed table of contents almost as soon as I begin fieldwork, I do not "think publication" with that same single-mindedness. Writing up qualitative research differs from most writing done for commercial publication. In commercial publication, contract negotiations usually precede the major part of the writing. In preparing a textbook, for example, it is not uncommon to invite an author to submit a proposed table of contents and a first chapter or two. In our work, the research act is not really finished until our studies are completed and accessible to others. The customary form for that documentation is a written account. When we set out to find a publisher, we ordinarily have a completed project in hand, not just an idea or prospectus.

I don't advise sending anything longer than a journal article to a publisher or editor without prior communication and an explicit request for more. If it is "common knowledge" that unsolicited manuscripts have only a slim chance of being published (Powell, 1985, p. 89), then the secret is to get a manuscript solicited. To solicit an invitation, send the title page and table of contents, accompanied by a carefully prepared letter (addressed to a particular individual by name, if possible) explaining why you have chosen the publisher and describing the status of the manuscript and any unusual circumstances surrounding it – such as how soon you could send a completed draft, or problems with clearances, ownership, or conditions surrounding publication. Although such blanket inquiries might be sent to several publishers, once you receive an indication of serious interest, stop playing the field. If you are tempted to browbeat publishers or journal editors by claiming that a manuscript is under consideration elsewhere, recognize that your ploy may backfire. Who wants to invest time and money in a go/no go decision on a manuscript that may be withdrawn summarily?

Journal publication seems the more realistic option for getting into print if you can pare down or parcel out a longer manuscript. Journal-length manuscripts move about easily among colleagues and editors. You do not need an invitation to submit a manuscript to a journal. About the only occasion when you might communicate with an editorial office prior to submission is when you are uncertain whether the content fits within a journal's scope or if an article presents some unusual problem such as requiring special graphics or exceeding customary length. Even in these cases, expect the reply, "Send it along and let us have a look at it." On the other hand, authors need to select journals with care and to demonstrate awareness not only to scope but to all stated requirements for submission.

A cover letter can provide a brief introduction and should also explain any aberration between the submission as made and the stated requirements of the journal. These requirements usually appear in every issue of professional journals under a heading like "Information for Authors." You must comply with major requirements, such as the number of copies to be submitted. Minor deviations should be acknowledged and explained—as, for example, recognizing that the citation style in the draft differs from that of the journal and will be corrected if the manuscript receives favorable review. A manuscript, however, should not be accompanied by an apology or a sweeping promise to do anything to get it accepted. Comply with the requirements and let the manuscript speak for itself, as it will have to do when published. Remember that editors of professional journals are, for the most part, busy academic researchers and teachers who must get on with their own work; they have every right to expect manuscripts to be in polished, proper, and final form (even if they subsequently ask for major revision).

Nobody relishes rejection. Having a manuscript rejected is always disappointing, to old-timers as well as new authors. The most difficult rejections are those that arrive without explanation or comment. Yet I know from having to pen such letters as an editor, and from having to make sure they will not be misinterpreted as giving false hope or phony encouragement, that at times there isn't anything to say except "Thank you for considering this journal."

In spite of efforts at multiple, external, and sometimes blind review, the referee process of professional journals can seem capricious. One problem is that final editorial decisions cannot rest solely on the basis of outside reviewers' recommendations. Accordingly, a rejection or two should not lead to a premature conclusion that an article is unworthy. But pay attention to any specific suggestions or criticisms offered with a rejection. I also think it a good idea to share a rejection letter with close colleagues; subtle messages between the lines sometimes escape sensitive authors.

Waiting for review provides another respite that can be turned to advantage. With the passing of time, one can usually return to a manuscript with a fresh look. If you are really brave, when your manuscript is returned, read it afresh as though you were a reviewer rather than the author.

I never read anything of my own in draft—no matter how long I have been working on it—without a pencil in hand, looking for sentences that can be shortened, ideas that can be expressed more clearly, or interpretations that can be strengthened. Once a manuscript is in production, however, my compulsive editing comes to an abrupt halt. When something I have written finally appears in print, I read it with whatever sense of accomplishment seems warranted, never with a sense of disappointment. Those are my words, my sentences, my ideas. (And, after all that work, they better be mine, just as I wrote them, unless I have been advised of any but the most minor of editorial changes.) I stand by them. At the time they represented my best shot.

On Not Getting Published

What if you are unable to publish your full account? Then, realizing that its appeal is limited, you draft a couple of shorter articles reporting aspects of the work, but you are unable to find a publishing outlet for them. Is that the end of the world? Or your career?

Well, not getting published may not do much for your career, but after spending three decades in university settings, I can report that I have never heard of an academic promotion or tenure decision based *solely* on someone's publication record. Failure to publish "enough" seems only a convenient peg on which to hang negative decisions. If you had access to the publication record of everyone promoted at most institutions of higher learning, I think you would be shocked at how little some people have published. (Presumably they contribute to their institutions in other ways. If everyone were busy writing, who would prepare the institutional reports, call all those meetings, coach the performers, or ration the travel money?)

True, in so-called research universities you must write, create, produce, or manage *something,* but it strikes me as unlikely—and certainly seems misguided—that anyone whose motivation for publishing stems only from a concern for tenure or promotion would turn to qualitative research. Such individuals should not be looking for alternative forms *of* research, but for alternatives *to* research that satisfy criteria for achievement and recognition. There are numerous alternatives through which honorable contributions can be made to scholarship: synthesis papers, problem statements, position papers, program descriptions, critical reviews, and annotated bibliographies. No doubt some, perhaps most, of your colleagues are publishing, but take a second look at how many are publishing original research. What you are reading here, for example, is experience-based and in a scholarly tradition, but it is not research. Despite such humble origins, I expect it to count in the Great World Series in the Sky where academic achievement is recorded.

Assuming that you are committed to qualitative research, however, I urge you forevermore to regard writing as a vital component of the *research* process, rather than as an activity inexorably linked with publishing. Whether or not you publish is in no way as critical to your role as a qualitative researcher as whether you complete your studies by writing them up. Qualitative/descriptive research must exist in some tangible, processed form accessible to others. Unpublished field notes are not enough. Comprehensive field reports drawn from notes, completed but unpublished papers, papers modestly reproduced under the aegis of your department, papers presented at conferences—all these *do* count toward scholarship and, as well, toward your credibility (and visibility) as a researcher who carries work to completion.

I include titles of some of my unpublished papers in my professional vita (separately from published ones—I'm not trying to pad, only to present a full account) and copies of them are available, should anyone ask. I mention them to graduate students who may not recognize that a successful career doesn't mean that every effort along the way is necessarily a success. Even success can impose a formidable barrier to further writing, especially if it comes with one's earliest publications. Those of us who have been at this awhile also hear the whispers that we no longer seem to write as well as we once did. Nor does every publication receive the recognition we might feel it deserves. We, too, have batting averages. Nobody scores a hit every time.

Thank goodness they don't. There's too much in print already. Not all our work needs to be published, certainly not in the slick format of expensive journals and books. For the most part, our purposes could be accomplished with less formal and expensive formats, such as in seminar papers modestly circulated to colleagues without the awkward accompanying question, "Where should I send this?" It would be nice if only the good stuff made it to the top and there was less of it. But that isn't realistic, and if we made a strong start in that direction we would soon be disagreeing about what constitutes the good stuff.

By all means stay with any worthwhile study until you have seen it through to the completion of a clearly conceptualized and well-written account. Make sure copies reach the hands of the people who share your research interests. Without insisting that you "must" get published, ask their advice in determining the audience you should reach and how much additional effort on your part seems needed and warranted. Published or not, you've written up your qualitative research. Your work wasn't completed until you did. Or, if not actually completed, at least it is a beginning, and that is something.

REFERENCES

Agar, Michael H. (1980) The Professional Stranger: An Informal Introduction to Ethnography. New York: Academic Press.

Bateson, Gregory (1936) Naven. Stanford, CA: Stanford University Press.

Becker, Howard S. (1986) Writing for Social Scientists: How to Start and Finish Your Thesis, Book, or Article. Chicago: University of Chicago Press.

Benedict, Ruth (1946) The Chrysanthemum and the Sword: Patterns of Japanese Culture. Boston: Houghton Mifflin.

Bernard, H. Russell (1988) Research Methods in Cultural Anthropology. Newbury Park, CA: Sage.

Burke, Kenneth (1935) Permanence and Change. New York: New Republic.

Clinton, Charles A. (1975) "The anthropologist as hired hand." Human Organization 34(2): 197-204.

Clinton, Charles A. (1976) "On bargaining with the devil: Contract ethnography and accountability in fieldwork." [Council on] Anthropology and Education Quarterly 7(2): 25-28.

Conrad, Peter and Shulamit Reinharz (eds.) (1984) "Computers and qualitative data." (Special Issue) Qualitative Sociology 7(1-2).

Crapanzano, Vincent (1980) Tuhami: Portrait of a Moroccan. Chicago: University of Chicago Press.

Elbow, Peter (1981) Writing with Power: Techniques for Mastering the Writing Process. New York: Oxford University Press.

Emerson, Robert M. and Melvin Pollner (1988) "On the uses of members' responses to researchers' accounts." Human Organization 47(3): 189-198.

Fetterman, David (1989) "Ethnographer as rhetorician: Multiple audiences reflect multiple realities." Practicing Anthropology 11(2): 2, 17-18.

Fitzsimmons, Stephen J. (1975) "The anthropologist in a strange land." Human Organization 34(2): 183-196.

Flower, Linda (1979) "Writer-based prose: A cognitive basis for problems in writing." College English 41: 19-37.

Flower, Linda and John R. Hayes (1981) "A cognitive process theory of writing." College Composition and Communication 32: 365-387.

Foster, George M. (1969) Applied Anthropology. Boston: Little, Brown.

Geertz, Clifford (1973) "Thick description," pp. 3-30 in Clifford Geertz (ed.) The Interpretation of Cultures. New York: Basic Books.

Geertz, Clifford (1988) Works and Lives: The Anthropologist as Author. Stanford, CA: Stanford University Press.

Heise, David R. (ed.) (1981) "Microcomputers in social research." (Special Issue) Sociological Methods and Research 9(4).

Keesing, Roger M. and Felix M. Keesing (1971) New Perspectives in Cultural Anthropology. New York: Holt, Rinehart & Winston.

Lewis, Oscar (1961) The Children of Sanchez: Autobiography of a Mexican Family. New York: Random House.

Lincoln, Yvonna and Egon Guba (1985) Naturalistic Inquiry. Beverly Hills, CA: Sage.

Lomask, Milton (1987) The Biographer's Craft. New York: Harper & Row.

Malinowski, Bronislaw (1922) Argonauts of the Western Pacific: An Account of Native Enterprise and Adventure in the Archipelagoes of Melanesian New Guinea. London: Routledge and Sons. (Reissued 1984 by Waveland Press)

Marcus, George E. and Michael M. Fischer (1986) Anthropology as Cultural Critique: An Experimental Moment in the Human Sciences. Chicago: University of Chicago Press.

McDermott, Ray (1976) Kids Make Sense: An Ethnographic Account of the Interactional Management of Success and Failure in One First-Grade Classroom. Unpublished doctoral dissertation, Stanford University.

Miles, Matthew B. and A. Michael Huberman (1984) Qualitative Data Analysis. Beverly Hills, CA: Sage.

Nash, Jeffrey (1990) "Working at and working: Computer fritters." Journal of Contemporary Ethnography 19(2): 207-225.

Noblit, George W. and R. Dwight Hare (1988) Meta-Ethnography: Synthesizing Qualitative Studies. Sage University Paper Series on Qualitative Research Methods, Vol. 11. Beverly Hills, CA: Sage.

Peacock, J. L. (1986) The Anthropological Lens: Harsh Light, Soft Focus. New York: Cambridge University Press.

Peshkin, Alan (1985) "From title to title: The evolution of perspective in naturalistic inquiry." Anthropology and Education Quarterly 16(3): 214-224.

Pfaffenberger, Bryan (1988) Microcomputer Applications in Qualitative Research. Sage University Paper Series on Qualitative Research Methods, Vol. 14. Beverly Hills, CA: Sage.

Powell, Walter W. (1985) Getting Into Print: The Decision-Making Process in Scholarly Publishing. Chicago: University of Chicago Press.

Rohner, Ronald P. (1975) They Love Me, They Love Me Not: A Worldwide Study of the Effects of Parental Acceptance and Rejection. New Haven, CT: HRAF Press.

Rohner, Ronald P. and Evelyn C. Rohner (1970) The Kwakiutl Indians of British Columbia. New York: Holt, Rinehart & Winston. (Reissued 1986 by Waveland Press)

Seidel, John V. and Jack A. Clark (1984) "THE ETHNOGRAPH: A computer program for the analysis of qualitative data." Qualitative Sociology 7(1-2): 110-125.

Shostak, Marjorie (1981) Nisa: The Life and Words of a !Kung Woman. New York: Random House.

Simmons, Leo W. (ed.) (1942) Sun Chief: The Autobiography of a Hopi Indian. New Haven, CT: Yale University Press.

Strunk, William, Jr., and E. B. White (1972) Elements of Style (2nd ed.). New York: Macmillan.

Taylor, Steven J., and Robert Bogdan (1984) Introduction to Qualitative Research Methods: The Search for Meanings (2nd ed.). New York: John Wiley.

Tufte, Edward R. (1983) The Visual Display of Quantitative Information. Cheshire, CT: Graphics Press.

Van Maanen, John (1988) Tales of the Field: On Writing Ethnography. Chicago: University of Chicago Press.

Wax, Murray L., Rosalie H. Wax, and Robert V. Dumont, Jr. (1964) "Formal education in an American Indian community." Supplement to Social Problems 11(4). (Reissued 1989 by Waveland Press)

Wax, Rosalie H. (1971) Doing Fieldwork: Warnings and Advice. Chicago: University of Chicago Press.

Whitehead, Alfred North (1949) The Aims of Education. New York: Mentor. (Originally published 1929)

Wolcott, Harry F. (1967) A Kwakiutl Village and School. New York: Holt, Rinehart & Winston. (Reissued 1989 by Waveland Press with a new Afterword)

Wolcott, Harry F. (1973) The Man in the Principal's Office: An Ethnography. New York: Holt, Rinehart & Winston. (Reissued 1984 by Waveland Press with a new Introduction)

Wolcott, Harry F. (1974) "The elementary school principal: Notes from a field study," pp. 176-204 in George D. Spindler (ed.) Education and Cultural Process: Toward an Anthropology of Education. New York: Holt, Rinehart & Winston. (Reissued 1987 by Waveland Press)

Wolcott, Harry F. (1975) "Introduction." (Special issue on the Ethnography of Schooling) Human Organization 34(2): 109-110.

Wolcott, Harry F. (1977) Teachers Versus Technocrats: An Educational Innovation in Anthropological Perspective. Eugene: Center for Educational Policy and Management, University of Oregon.

Wolcott, Harry F. (1982) "Differing styles of on-site research, or, 'if it isn't ethnography, what is it?' " Review Journal of Philosophy and Social Science 7(1, 2): 154-169.

Wolcott, Harry F. (1983a) "Adequate schools and inadequate education: The life history of a sneaky kid." Anthropology and Education Quarterly 14(1): 3-32.

Wolcott, Harry F. (1983b) "A Malay village that progress chose: Sungai Lui and the Institute of Cultural Affairs." Human Organization 42(1): 72-81.

Wolcott, Harry F. (1987) "On ethnographic intent," pp. 37-57 in George and Louise Spindler (eds.) Interpretive Ethnography of Education. Hillsdale, NJ: Lawrence Erlbaum.

Wolcott, Harry F. (1988) "Problem finding in qualitative research," pp. 11-35 in Henry Trueba and C. Delgado-Gaitan (eds.) School and Society: Learning Content Through Culture. New York: Praeger.

Wolcott, Harry F. (1990a) "Making a study 'more ethnographic.' " (Special Issue: The Presentation of Ethnographic Research) Journal of Contemporary Ethnography 19(1): 44-72.

Wolcott, Harry F. (1990b) "On seeking—and rejecting—validity in qualitative research," pp. 121-152 in Elliot W. Eisner and Alan Peshkin (eds.) Qualitative Inquiry in Education: The Continuing Debate. New York: Teachers College Press.

Woods, Peter (1985) "New songs played skilfully: Creativity and technique in writing up qualitative research," pp. 86-106 in Robert G. Burgess (ed.) Issues in Educational Research: Qualitative Methods. Philadelphia, PA: Falmer.

ABOUT THE AUTHOR/ABOUT THE MONOGRAPH

HARRY F. WOLCOTT is Professor of Education and Anthropology at the University of Oregon. After completing his Ph. D. at Stanford in 1964, he accepted a position at Oregon, intending to remain "a couple of years." A quarter of a century later he's still there, having published "several books and numerous articles on a wide variety of topics." Whether he has natural talent as a writer is not known; few have ever seen his early drafts. That many of his publications remain in print or have been republished suggests that he does attend to revising and editing with considerable care, as former secretaries will attest but now only his trusty personal computer knows for sure. He has served as guest editor and editor-in-chief of professional journals in anthropology, sociology, and education.

The invitation to prepare a monograph on writing was extended by Acquisitions Editor Mitch Allen of Sage Publications. The completed draft was greeted with encouragement, enthusiasm, and insightful comment by Series Editor John Van Maanen. Their suggestions were coupled with timely critical readings by students, friends, and colleagues, with special thanks to C. H. Edson, David Flinders, Anna Kohner, Jan Lewis, Tom Schram, George D. Spindler, Robert K. Wilson, and Philip D. Young. The genius of computers, coupled in this case with the patient instruction of Leslie Conery, have made one more convert for word processing as an indispensable tool in writing up research.

NOTES

NOTES